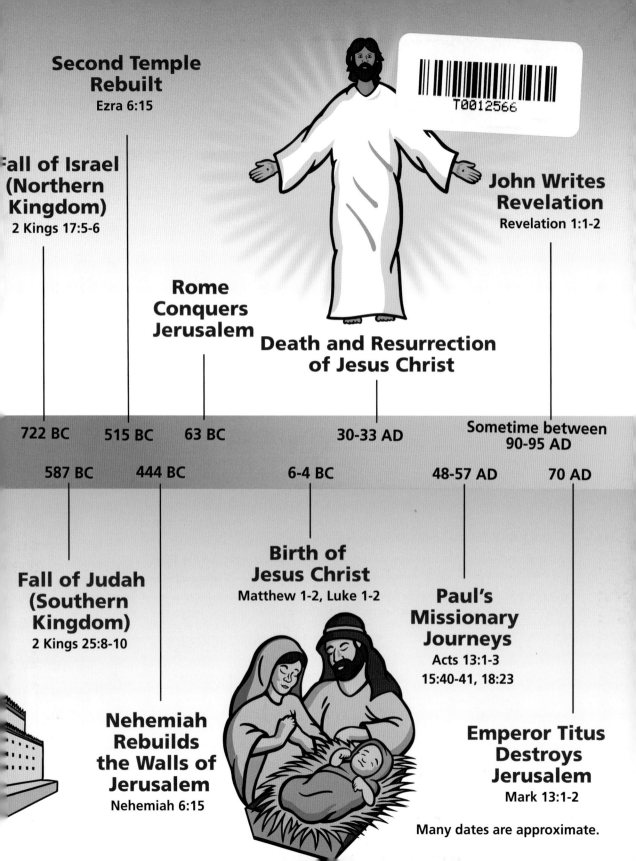

Second Temple Rebuilt
Ezra 6:15

Fall of Israel (Northern Kingdom)
2 Kings 17:5-6

John Writes Revelation
Revelation 1:1-2

Rome Conquers Jerusalem

Death and Resurrection of Jesus Christ

722 BC    515 BC    63 BC              30-33 AD        Sometime between 90-95 AD

587 BC    444 BC         6-4 BC              48-57 AD    70 AD

Birth of Jesus Christ
Matthew 1-2, Luke 1-2

Fall of Judah (Southern Kingdom)
2 Kings 25:8-10

Paul's Missionary Journeys
Acts 13:1-3
15:40-41, 18:23

Nehemiah Rebuilds the Walls of Jerusalem
Nehemiah 6:15

Emperor Titus Destroys Jerusalem
Mark 13:1-2

Many dates are approximate.

T0012566

ZONDERKIDZ

*Adventure Bible Guide*
Copyright © 2024 by Zondervan

Published in Grand Rapids, Michigan, by Zonderkidz. Zonderkidz is a registered trademark of The Zondervan Corporation, L.L.C., a wholly owned subsidary of HarperCollins Christian Publishing, Inc.

Requests for information should be addressed to customercare@harpercollins.com.

Library of Congress Cataloging-in-Publication Data

Names: Zonderkidz, editor.
Title: The adventure Bible guide : explore the stories, people, and places of every book in the Bible / [edited by] Zonderkidz.
Description: Grand Rapids : Zonderkidz, [2024] | Audience: Ages 8-12 | Summary: "Explore the Bible like never before! This companion to the bestselling Adventure Bible gives young readers the key details of every book of the Bible at their fingertips. With kid-friendly overviews of Genesis through Revelation and full-color infographics, maps, and images, children will strengthen their faith and gain a better understanding of the most important story ever told"-- Provided by publisher.
Identifiers: LCCN 2023037637 (print) | LCCN 2023037638 (ebook) | ISBN 9780310156048 (hardcover) | ISBN 9780310156062 (ebook)
Subjects: LCSH: Bible stories, English--Juvenile literature. | Bible--Juvenile literature. | BISAC: JUVENILE NONFICTION / Religion / Biblical Reference | JUVENILE NONFICTION / Religious / Christian / Learning Concepts
Classification: LCC BS551.3 .A345 2024 (print) | LCC BS551.3 (ebook) | DDC 220.95/05--dc23/eng/20240110
LC record available at https://lccn.loc.gov/2023037637
LC ebook record available at https://lccn.loc.gov/2023037638

Zondervan titles may be purchased in bulk for educational, business, fundraising, or sales promotional use. For information, please email SpecialMarkets@Zondervan.com.

*Cover Illustration: Kevin Keele*
*Interior Illustrations: Brian Oesch*
*Interior Design: Denise Froehlich*
*Written by Nancy I. Sanders*

*Printed in India*

24 25 26 27 28 / REP / 10 9 8 7 6 5 4 3 2 1

# Adventure BIBLE GUIDE

EXPLORE THE STORIES, PEOPLE, AND PLACES OF EVERY BOOK IN THE BIBLE

 ZONDER**kidz**

# Genesis

Genesis is the first book of the Bible, and it's about beginnings. Most importantly, it's the beginning of a wonderful plan. Before God created anything, he had you in mind. He wanted to be with you, walk with you, and talk with you forever. With you on his heart, he created the universe. He set his plan in motion to send Jesus, the Savior of the world. He started history so you could be part of his forever! Let's get started on our exciting adventure through the books of the Bible, which show us how we can live with God . . . forever!

## Choices

Do people automatically love God? No. That wouldn't be real love. Did God program us to only do good and not evil? No. That would make us robots. God created people in his own image to think, choose, and make decisions. God gave us free will because he wants us to *choose* to love and obey him. Genesis traces the history of the first man and woman and the generations that came after. We learn about the choices they made—good and bad. As a loving, just, and wise heavenly father, God deals with each choice we make too . . . in the right way.

Jacob, Joseph, Isaac, Abraham, and Noah are just some of the people we learn about in Genesis. Other people to look for include Adam and Eve, Cain and Abel and Seth, Sarah, Rebekah, Leah and Rachel, and Judah.

iStock.com/sedmak

## Promises

The Bible is filled with God's promises! Here are three from Genesis.

1. God promised Adam and Eve he'd send a Savior who will crush the power of evil forever (Genesis 3:14–15).
2. God promised Noah he'd never again send a flood to destroy the earth. The rainbow is a reminder of this promise (Genesis 9:8–17).
3. God promised Abraham he'd give Abraham's children's children the land of Canaan and bless the entire world through him (Genesis 12:1–3 and 15:1–7).

Did God fulfill his promises? Of course! He always does! Keep reading the rest of the Bible. You'll discover promises God made for us too!

## Days of Creation

**Day One:**
God made light.

**Day Two:**
God made sky and water.

**Day Three:**
God made seas, land, and plants.

**Day Four:**
God made the sun, moon, and stars.

**Day Five:**
God made fish and birds.

**Day Six:**
God made land animals and humans.

ZZZZZZZZZZZZ

**Day Seven:**
God rested.

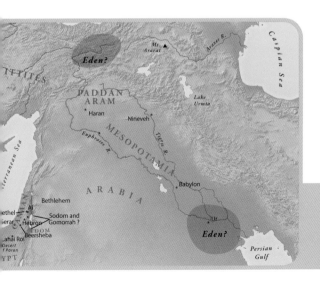

We can't be quite sure where the Bible lands were located before Noah and the flood, but after the waters dried up, this is the part of the world where events in Genesis took place.

# Exodus

The word *exodus* is used when a large group of people permanently leave somewhere together. The book of Exodus tells us how the Israelites left Egypt to start their journey to the promised land. Their leader? Moses. Born a Hebrew (another word for Israelite), he was raised as an Egyptian prince. The first part of Exodus is about Moses's life, the Israelites' slavery in Egypt, and how God set them free from captivity. The second part is about God showing the Hebrews who he is as their God. He called them to obey the Ten Commandments, build a place of worship, and follow him and his ways.

## Moses, the Author

Scholars agree Moses recorded God's important laws for the Israelites, which are found in the first five books of the Bible—things such as the Ten Commandments, the Levitical law, and how the Israelites should live and worship.

Pharaoh's daughter found Moses and raised him in Egypt's courts as her son. Moses might have grown up thinking he would one day become pharaoh. Instead, God chose Moses to lead the Israelites.

*The Finding of Moses* by Lawrence Alma-Tadema, 1904. Public domain.

## A Nation Is Born

The events in Exodus continue the history that began in Genesis. In this book, we discover how the nation of Israel was born. It started when God promised Abraham his descendants would become a mighty nation in Genesis 12:1–3. It continued through one family—Abraham's grandson Jacob had twelve sons who later moved to Egypt. Their descendants became slaves under different pharaohs (Egyptian kings) for generations, and they multiplied into hundreds of thousands of

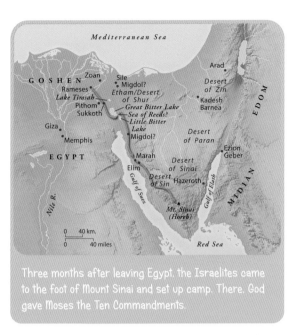

Three months after leaving Egypt, the Israelites came to the foot of Mount Sinai and set up camp. There, God gave Moses the Ten Commandments.

people. God used a series of miraculous events to set them free. While wandering in the desert, they changed from a fearful and oppressed people into a nation of mighty warriors.

## The Ten Plagues of Egypt

The story of Moses meeting with Pharaoh to set the Hebrews free is one of the most famous parts of the Bible. Even if we don't understand why God chose those ten terrible plagues, we can trust he did what was needed at just the right time to punish Egypt. As you read, look for these plagues as well as other things God did to take care of his chosen people.

In the New Testament, the Pharisees asked Jesus which was the greatest commandment. Jesus referred to the first four of the Ten Commandments when he said the greatest was to love God. Then Jesus referred to the remaining six commandments when he added the second greatest was to love other people. Read Exodus 20:1–17 and Matthew 22:36–40 to learn more.

### The Ten Plagues of Egypt

1. Water into blood
2. Frogs
3. Gnats
4. Flies
5. Death of livestock
6. Boils
7. Hail
8. Locusts
9. Darkness
10. Death of the firstborn

# Leviticus

Offerings. Sacrifices. Feasts. Leviticus lists instructions God told Moses for worshiping and walking with him. Now that the Israelites were no longer slaves in Egypt, they had a lot to learn about being a nation. They also had a lot to learn about following Yahweh, the one true God. This book records the rules and laws and best decisions for every part of their lives—all given by God himself!

## Holiness

Leviticus can be divided into two major parts. The first part explains the sacrifices the people offered to a holy God. The second part explains how to live a holy life.

© by Zondervan

All the Israelites gathered at the tabernacle for a special ceremony to consecrate the priests and set them apart as holy workers for God. Leviticus lists many instructions the priests had to follow for offerings and sacrifices.

## Seven Feasts

In Leviticus, there are instructions for celebrating seven holy holidays each year.

**Passover** remembered when the angel of death passed over the families of Israel during the final plague, and the firstborn Israelites were protected because of an innocent lamb's blood.

**Festival of Unleavened Bread** remembered how the Israelites left Egypt quickly.

**Offering the Firstfruits** was a time to thank God at the beginning of the harvest.

**Festival of Weeks**, also called **Pentecost**, celebrated the harvest and remembered when God gave them the Ten Commandments.

**Festival of Trumpets** was celebrated with trumpet blasts and offerings.

**Day of Atonement** was a time for the people to remember their sins and ask for forgiveness.

**Festival of Tabernacles** remembered God's presence when they wandered in the wilderness.

# The Tabernacle

**The tabernacle was made from animal skin and curtains.**

golden lampstand

Most Holy Place

Holy Place

ark of the covenant

altar of incense

table for the bread of the Presence

bronze basin

altar of burnt offering

## The Tabernacle

God spoke to Moses from the tabernacle, the place of worship. Also called the tent of meeting, it was portable and could be carried by the Israelites as they traveled through the desert. While living in slavery, the Israelites had become the builders, craft workers, and artists of Egypt. They used these skills to build the tabernacle. Outside the tabernacle was an altar where priests could burn the offerings and sacrifices people brought. The furniture inside included a seven-branched gold lampstand, a table for the holy bread, and the ark of the covenant.

## A Call for Holiness

The Israelites needed to learn that, unlike the gods of Egypt, God is holy. Leviticus was a call for God's people to be holy too. These instructions taught them to bring God animal sacrifices for their sins and ask forgiveness for the wrong things they did. With his death on the cross, Jesus paid the ultimate sacrifice for our sins. Now animal sacrifices are no longer needed when we tell God we're sorry and ask for his forgiveness.

### Did You Know?

The ark of the covenant was the most holy object the Israelites possessed. It was a wooden box covered with gold that had important things like the Ten Commandments inside. But it wasn't just a fancy box. The presence of God was there.

# Numbers

The Israelites were at Mount Sinai when God ordered a census. Moses and Aaron were given the task of counting the number of men old enough to go to war. God commanded another census forty years later, when the Israelites camped near Jericho. Once again, they counted the number of soldiers who would make up their army. That's one reason this book is called Numbers.

## A Short Distance in a Long Time

This book is also about the number of years it took the Israelites to get from Mount Sinai to Jericho. At about 345 miles, it takes less than a day to travel there by car today.[1] But it took the Israelites forty years. Why? Because the men and women who left Egypt doubted God, God said they couldn't see the land he was giving them. But their children learned to trust in God and were ready to follow him into the promised land.

A.D. Riddle/BiblePlaces.com

There was one road running north and south through the region east of the Dead Sea, called the King's Highway. The Israelites asked neighboring kingdoms if they could travel along this road for part of their journey. You can still travel along the King's Highway today!

## The Covenant

Hundreds of years earlier, God made a covenant, or lasting agreement, with Abraham. God picked Abraham's family to be his chosen people and promised to give them the land of Canaan. In return, Abraham promised to worship only God. When God brought the Israelites—Abraham's family—out of Egypt, he led them to the land from this covenant.

This ancient silver piece has the same blessing as Numbers 6:24–26 written on it. It's the oldest example of this phrase ever found— dating from the seventh century BC.

## The Cloud

A cloud covered the tabernacle each day. It showed the Israelites the presence of God was with them. At night, the cloud lit up like fire. When the cloud moved, the Israelites packed up and followed it. When the cloud stopped, the Israelites camped in that place.

## The Trumpets

How do you move an entire nation from one camp to the next? God told Moses to make two silver trumpets. Different signals meant different commands. The Israelites knew by listening to the trumpet blasts which tribes should start moving and when.

## Faith Is a Choice

Some people today argue that if they could see God do a miracle, they would believe in him, obey his commandments, and follow his holy ways. Numbers tells us the first generation of Israelites witnessed God's mighty power numerous times . . . and still chose not to believe! These examples remind us faith is a choice. We can choose to believe in God because of who he is, not what he does for us.

# Deuteronomy

In Deuteronomy, Moses assembled the Israelites and gave three important farewell speeches. What did Moses talk about? God's covenant with Israel. All the Israelites except Joshua and Caleb had been children when Moses got the Ten Commandments at Mount Sinai. That was forty years earlier. Now these children were grown. Moses reminded the new generation about God, his commandments, and the blessings they would receive if they chose to follow God and his holy ways.

## Moses, God's Leader

In Deuteronomy, we hear speeches from Moses and learn about his death. Moses was 120 years old when he died. Even though he didn't take the Israelites into the promised land, Moses was one of the most important leaders the nation of Israel ever had.

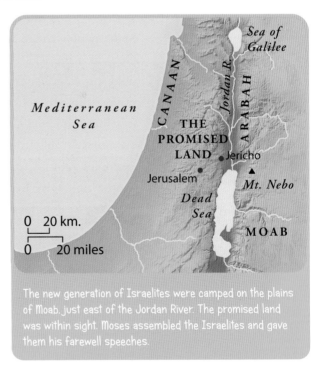

The new generation of Israelites were camped on the plains of Moab, just east of the Jordan River. The promised land was within sight. Moses assembled the Israelites and gave them his farewell speeches.

While Moses and the Israelites looked out over the promised land, the people who lived there were looking back at them. What were they thinking? This clay tablet and hundreds like it are known as the Amarna letters, and some seem to refer to the Hebrews attacking. They say the Canaanites were afraid as they witnessed an army begin to conquer the land.

## The Ten Commandments

The Ten Commandments were not given by a cruel tyrant to threaten or punish us. They were given by a loving Father who knows what's best for his children. The Ten Commandments teach us right from wrong, but they're more than that. They show we need a Savior. Because we can't follow these rules on our own and sometimes sin, God sent Jesus to offer us forgiveness when we repent of our sin and tell God we're sorry. Write the Ten Commandments on your heart so you learn how God wants us to live.

Public domain. Courtesy of The Metropolitan Museum.

### The Ten Commandments

1. Love God most of all.
2. Worship God alone, not an image or idol.
3. Always speak God's name with respect.
4. Follow God's example to take a holy day of rest.
5. Honor your father and mother with love and respect.
6. Value life and do not murder anyone.
7. Stay faithful to your husband or wife after you are married.
8. Don't steal something that isn't yours.
9. Always speak the truth.
10. Be content, not jealous for something someone else has.

# Joshua

The book of Joshua begins with the transfer of leadership from Moses to Joshua. After Moses died, God gave Joshua instructions on taking command. This book has two main parts. The first part is about conquering the land of Canaan. The second part is about dividing up the land among the twelve tribes of Israel and settling down to live in the promised land.

## Meet Joshua!

Joshua was Moses's assistant. He hiked up Mount Sinai when Moses received the Ten Commandments. He obeyed God the entire forty years the Israelites wandered in the wilderness. After Moses died, Joshua was appointed Israel's new leader. How did Joshua feel? Probably scared! Then God spoke to him, telling him not to be afraid. God reminded Joshua to be strong and take courage because God would be with him. Always remember: God promises to be with you, just as he promised to be with Joshua. God also encouraged Joshua. As you read, look for ways God wants to encourage you too!

## So Many Questions

People have questions about this book. How could God, who is loving and good, send the Israelites into Canaan to destroy their cities? It might have been because

The promised land was divided among the tribes of Israel. But the tribe of Levi didn't receive a plot of land. Instead, the Levites were given cities and fields within each of the other tribes' lands so they were spread among the people and could help teach them about God and his holy laws.

the Canaanites did terrible sins, and this was their punishment. God allowed the Israelites to be conquered too, years later, when they were worshiping other gods.

In heaven, we will find out the actual answers to our questions. They will be perfect. That's because we know God is perfect, loving, good, and wise, even when we don't understand his ways.

## Rahab Chooses God

The Canaanites heard about the victories God gave the Israelites and trembled in fear. Rahab, however, made the choice to trust God. She hid two Israelite spies, then secretly helped them escape over Jericho's city wall (Joshua 2:1–16). Later, she married Salmon, one of the Israelites. They had a son named Boaz, whose great-grandson was King David. His descendant was Jesus. In the New Testament, Rahab is included in Jesus's family tree (see Matthew 1:2–16)!

Jericho was surrounded by a wall. In ancient times, many cities had walls built around them to protect their people from attacks.

Balage Balogh, archaelogyillustrated.com

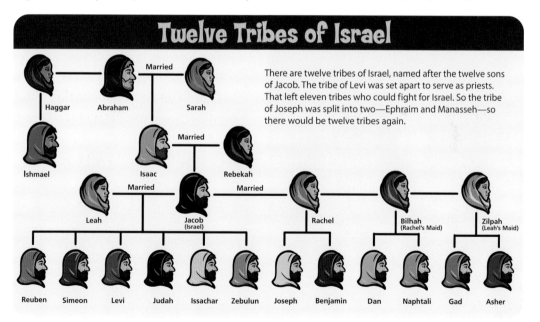

# Twelve Tribes of Israel

There are twelve tribes of Israel, named after the twelve sons of Jacob. The tribe of Levi was set apart to serve as priests. That left eleven tribes who could fight for Israel. So the tribe of Joseph was split into two—Ephraim and Manasseh—so there would be twelve tribes again.

Haggar    Abraham    Married    Sarah

Ishmael    Isaac    Married    Rebekah

Leah    Married    Jacob (Israel)    Married    Rachel    Bilhah (Rachel's Maid)    Zilpah (Leah's Maid)

Reuben    Simeon    Levi    Judah    Issachar    Zebulun    Joseph    Benjamin    Dan    Naphtali    Gad    Asher

# Judges

The Israelites followed God during Joshua's lifetime. But the next generation didn't grow up seeing the mighty deeds God had done for Israel. They worshiped their neighbors' gods instead. Judges tells what happened after the Israelites settled in Canaan. It was a time when God raised up leaders called judges. These judges helped govern the Israelites. Some judges delivered them from enemy armies. Some called them to repent and turn back to God.

## The Court of Deborah

Deborah was one of Israel's judges. People came to her with problems and she judged their cases. When Barak, Israel's general, asked Deborah to join him in leading their troops to battle, she agreed. Jabin, one of the Canaanite kings, had nine hundred iron chariots and had oppressed the Israelites for twenty years. But on the day Deborah and Barak led the battle against him, God gave Israel the victory. Nothing can stop God's power!

## The Story of Samson

Samson was a very strong man. God gave him his special strength, but Samson did not always make wise choices and often disobeyed God's laws. Even though Samson was far from perfect, God still used him as a judge. Samson made a heroic sacrifice for his nation when he knocked down the temple where Israel's enemies, the Philistines, worshiped their false god.

Historia/Shutterstock.com

Gideon, one of Israel's judges, led their army to an amazing victory against the Midianites. Gideon wasn't always a fearless leader, though. In fact, he felt like the weakest person in Israel. God called him, encouraged him, and strengthened him. And Gideon learned an important lesson: When God helps you to stand up and be brave, the victory comes from him! Read Judges 6:11–7:22 to learn more.

## The Goodness of God

God made a covenant with Israel to bless them if they worshiped him. But Israel sinned by worshiping other gods and following their evil practices. God, in his goodness and wisdom, allowed Israel's enemies to oppress them. Many times, that reminded Israel to turn back to God for his help.

As you read through Judges, look for these important lessons:

© 1995 Phoenix Data Systems

In Old Testament times, the Philistines were skilled in working with iron, which made their armies very powerful.

1. God wants us to choose to do good things and obey the Bible's teachings.
2. If we sin, we can tell God we're sorry and ask for forgiveness.
3. We can ask God for help when we need it.

## Right From Wrong

In Judges, everyone did whatever they felt was right. Unfortunately, because they didn't look to God's words and laws for guidance, they often did the wrong thing. We don't have to make the same mistake. When you want to know right from wrong, look in the Bible to see what God says to do. Then do it! Ask God to give you strength to obey his word.

### The Judges of Israel

The book of Judges lists different judges in the early days of Israel's history. These judges served to settle arguments among the people as well as lead armies against their enemies.

1. Othniel
2. Ehud
3. Shamgar
4. Deborah
5. Gideon
6. Tola
7. Jair
8. Jephthah
9. Ibzan
10. Elon
11. Abdon
12. Samson
13. Samuel

# Ruth

The book of Ruth takes place during the time of the judges. Judges shows how Israel was often unfaithful to God, but Ruth shows there were still people who stayed faithful during these years. The main people in this book remained strong in their faith even in hard times.

## Let's Meet Ruth

Ruth lived in Moab, a country to the east of Israel. Moab and Israel were enemies at times. One day, newcomers came to Ruth's town. Naomi, her husband, and their two sons were Israelites from the town of Bethlehem. They had left Israel because of a terrible famine. Naomi and her family settled down in Moab. Ruth married Naomi's son, but all too soon, Naomi's husband and two sons died. When Naomi decided to move back to Bethlehem because the famine was over, Ruth went with her. Ruth declared to her mother-in-law that Naomi's people would now be her own people and the God of Israel would be her God.

## A Kinsman *What?*

Boaz was the kinsman-redeemer of Ruth. He was her *kinsman*, another word for relative. (He was related to Ruth through her mother-in-law, Naomi.) Boaz was also her

Jean-François Millet, *The Gleaners*. iStock.com/duncan1890

*redeemer*, which means to buy something back or free it. One responsibility of a kinsman-redeemer as a widow's relative was to buy the property of her dead husband. The kinsman-redeemer was also responsible to marry the widow so the name and property would be kept in the family, which is exactly what Boaz did with Ruth.

To feed herself and her mother-in-law, Ruth gathered barley and wheat from Boaz's fields during harvest time. This painting shows women gleaning in a similar way.

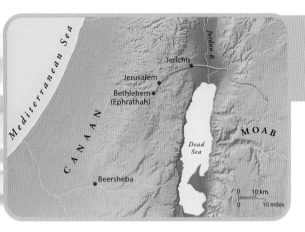

The book of Ruth follows a family whose journey started in Bethlehem, continued on to Moab, then ended back in Bethlehem. This map shows a possible route they took.

## Ruth and Rahab

Like Rahab in the book of Joshua, Ruth was not an Israelite. Like Rahab, Ruth heard about the God of Israel. And like Rahab, Ruth gave up her people's false gods and wanted God to be her God. Most special of all, just like Rahab, God chose Ruth to be part of Jesus's family tree! Rahab was Boaz's mother, Ruth's second mother-in-law.

## Bethlehem

The small town of Bethlehem became one of the most important places in the Bible. Ruth married Boaz here and started a family. King David, Ruth's great-grandson, was born here. And here, as predicted by the prophet Micah years later, the Messiah was born!

## Jesus's Family Tree

Salmon — Rahab

Boaz — Ruth

Obed

Jesse

David — Bathsheba

Solomon

You can read about Jesus's family tree in Ruth 4:18-22 and Matthew 1:1-17.

Jesus

# 1 Samuel

Israel's final judge was Samuel, the prophet. The book of 1 Samuel covers this time in Israel's history and how they demanded a king. God let them have one, and Saul was proclaimed king and sat on the throne. This book also introduces a youth named David. Unlike Saul, who disobeyed God, David followed after God with all his heart. God chose David to be the next king of Israel. Get ready for excitement: Giants! Battles! Adventure! You can read how it all happened—here in 1 Samuel!

## Bible Stories

Remember those Bible stories you heard when you were little? They weren't just stories. They were history! A lot of them can be found in this book. As you read through 1 Samuel, which stories can you remember hearing before?

## Who Were the Philistines?

One of Israel's toughest enemies were a group called the Philistines, who settled on the eastern shores of the Mediterranean Sea. The Philistines were richer than the Israelites. They knew how to make things from iron, but kept the process a secret from Israel, so their weapons were stronger too. They used these advantages during the time of the judges and Samuel to fight against the Israelites, capture their cities, and take their land.

The Philistines lived along the coast of the Mediterranean Sea.

## David's Parents

Six years or so after defeating Goliath, David was in danger. Because King Saul thought the people wanted David to be king instead of him, he plotted to kill David. David hid in a cave so Saul couldn't find him. When people heard about it, many joined David, and soon he had four hundred soldiers under his command. David's family joined him too. But Israel wasn't a safe place, especially for his mom and dad. David asked the king of Moab if his parents could stay in Moab for a while, where it was safe. Why Moab? David's great-grandmother, Ruth, was from Moab. Maybe their family still had connections there.

A.D. Riddle/BiblePlaces.com

Samuel anointed both Saul and David, the first two kings of Israel. Oil used for anointing was often carried in the hollowed-out horn of an animal.

jgroup/Getty images

Shepherds typically used a sling with stones to guard their sheep from lions or bears. David used his skill with this weapon to fight against the mighty giant Goliath, but he trusted in God to give him victory.

## Things to Look for in 1 Samuel

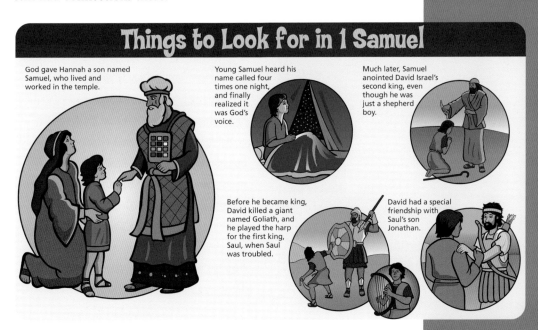

God gave Hannah a son named Samuel, who lived and worked in the temple.

Young Samuel heard his name called four times one night, and finally realized it was God's voice.

Much later, Samuel anointed David Israel's second king, even though he was just a shepherd boy.

Before he became king, David killed a giant named Goliath, and he played the harp for the first king, Saul, when Saul was troubled.

David had a special friendship with Saul's son Jonathan.

# 2 Samuel

The book of 2 Samuel is a history book. It describes the events that happened in Israel during the forty years King David ruled the country. It is also a biography of David's life—how he became king, how he established Jerusalem as his capital city, and how he won important battles against Israel's enemies. It is also a book of faith. Second Samuel shows us David's spiritual journey and how he sought to have a relationship with God with all his heart.

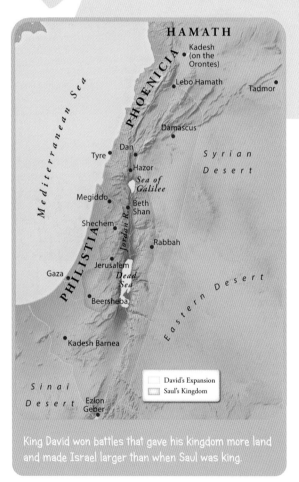

King David won battles that gave his kingdom more land and made Israel larger than when Saul was king.

## Learning from David

King David was close to God. Yet he still disobeyed God's laws and sinned. As you read about David's life in 2 Samuel, watch for these guidelines on what to do about sin.

### Lessons from David

1. Listen to God's Word so you know right from wrong. (David listened to the prophet Nathan. Today, we can read the Bible.)
2. When you sin, you can tell God you're sorry and ask for his forgiveness.
3. God always forgives you when you sincerely ask him.
4. Make changes so you don't do the same sin again. Ask God to help you.
5. Sometimes sin has consequences, and you might have hard times because of the choices you made, even though God has forgiven you.
6. The Bible says everyone sins. This shows everyone needs a Savior, no matter how hard they try to be perfect on their own.

## Israel's Second King

King Saul and his son Jonathan were killed in battle. The twelve tribes of Israel needed a new king. The tribe of Judah anointed David as their king because he was a member of their tribe. The other eleven tribes made Saul's son Ish-Bosheth their king. There was war between the two kingdoms until Ish-Bosheth was killed. Then the eleven tribes asked David to rule over them, making him king of all Israel.

Some Bible scholars used to wonder if David was a real hero, because no information about him had been found anywhere outside the Bible. But one day a stone was found that said "[Jehoram kin]g of the House of David" was killed in battle. Archaeological finds like this help show us our faith is founded on true events in history, not myths or fairy tales.

## The Covenant of David

In 2 Samuel 7:4–17, God sent David a special message through the prophet Nathan. God promised that after David died, one of David's descendants would be king forever. We know God was telling David that the Messiah would come though David's family tree. Plus, now we know the name of this forever king . . . Jesus!

King David Loved God. He spent Time praying and Talking with God. He also played a small harp and sang songs of praise and worship To God.

# 1 Kings

The books of 1 Kings and 2 Kings together tell the history of Israel from David's death on through the destruction of Jerusalem. In 1 Kings, we learn that after David died, his son Solomon became king. This was known as the golden age of Israel because King Solomon had many riches and built a temple of gold to worship God. After Solomon, the kingdom became divided, with Israel in the north and Judah in the south. Many kings in both the northern kingdom and the southern kingdom led the people into sin by worshiping other gods. Yet some kings, prophets, and people remained faithful to God even during these years. The book of 1 Kings tells the history of these times.

## Wise King, Unwise Choices

One night, God appeared to Solomon in a dream and asked him what he wanted most. Solomon said he wanted wisdom and understanding to rule over his people. Because Solomon asked for such a humble gift, God granted his request. But later Solomon did something that wasn't very wise: he married women who didn't believe in God. They worshiped other gods and soon persuaded Solomon to worship their gods too.

Even though you're not old enough to get married, you can still choose your friends. As you read through 1 Kings, look for guidelines on the choices God wants us to make. See the list on the next page for some examples.

erostunova/123RF.com

This carving depicts Elijah in a mighty victory over the prophets of Baal. Fire came down from heaven to show everyone that God alone is Lord!

1. Ask God for wisdom, especially when it comes to your friendships and getting along with others.
2. If your friends make good choices, stick with them! It will be easier for you to make good choices too.
3. If your friends do the wrong things, pray for them. Don't make the same mistake Solomon made and start doing the wrong things they do.
4. If you're having any problems with your friends, share them with trusted adults who love God. God sent prophets to help guide the kings of Israel, and he wants to help you too.

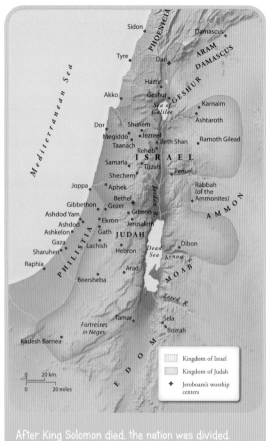

After King Solomon died, the nation was divided. Judah, the southern kingdom, was made up of the tribes of Judah and Benjamin. Its capital city was Jerusalem. The other ten tribes were known as Israel, the northern kingdom. Samaria eventually became its capital city.

A.D. Riddle/BiblePlaces.com

Using his riches, King Solomon did a lot of building in Israel. This limestone column was found in Jerusalem and could have been part of his construction projects.

## Kings and a Prophet

When the kings of Israel and Judah disobeyed God's laws, God sent prophets to teach them right from wrong. One of the most important prophets was Elijah. He preached God's messages to King Ahab and his son King Ahaziah. And when Elijah prayed, God made miracles happen!

# 2 Kings

The book of 2 Kings is all about . . . kings! It continues the history that began in 1 Kings about the rulers of the divided kingdoms of Israel and Judah. Second Kings also documents big changes in world powers during those years. Both Egypt and Syria tried to conquer the Hebrews. Then the Assyrian Empire attempted to dominate the world. After that, the Babylonian Empire took control, led by King Nebuchadnezzar. Ultimately, however, it is God who reigns! All nations must answer to him.

## God Is Righteous and Just

One of the biggest messages in 2 Kings is how God is righteous and just—he punishes evil and rewards good. Sometimes that judgment is easy to see. First, God allowed the northern kingdom of Israel to be conquered by the Assyrian Empire. That was punishment for their nineteen kings in a row who did evil deeds and led the people into sin. Next, God allowed the southern kingdom of Judah to be conquered by the Babylonian Empire, and Jerusalem was destroyed. That was punishment for the many times Judah's kings worshiped the vile gods of their neighbors. Sometimes judgment waits, however, and we don't see evil getting the punishment it deserves. But just because we don't see it doesn't mean it won't happen. The Bible tells us there will be a day of judgment when Jesus comes to earth to reign as king forever.

Giuseppe Angeli, *Elijah Taken Up in a Chariot of Fire*. Public domain.

The prophet Elijah spoke God's messages to the kingdom of Israel during the reigns of King Ahab and his son, King Ahaziah. Elijah did not die—he was carried up to heaven in a chariot of fire. Elisha took his place.

## Signs and Warnings

All through the reigns of kings in both the northern and southern kingdoms, God did not abandon his children. When they sinned, God sent prophets and priests with warnings and signs to guide them back to him. When people refused to turn from their evil ways, God warned them that punishment would come. He also promised that one day he would restore them back to himself.

Historia/Shutterstock.com

The priest Jehoiada and his wife protected the king's son Joash from a murderous plot when he was a year old, then six years later presented him as the king of Judah.

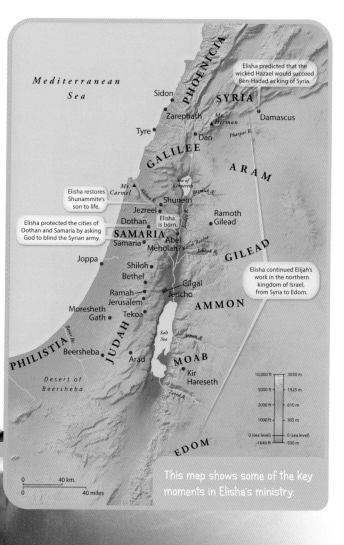

Elisha predicted that the wicked Hazael would succeed Ben-Hadad as king of Syria.

Elisha restores Shunammite's son to life.

Elisha protected the cities of Dothan and Samaria by asking God to blind the Syrian army.

Elisha continued Elijah's work in the northern kingdom of Israel, from Syria to Edom.

*Mediterranean Sea*

PHOENICIA
SYRIA
Sidon
Zarephath
Mt. Hermon
Damascus
Tyre
Dan
Pharpar R.
GALILEE
ARAM
Mt. Carmel
Sea of Kinnereth
Kishon R.
Yarmuk R.
Shunem
Jezreel
Elisha is born.
Ramoth Gilead
Dothan
Jordan R.
SAMARIA
Samaria
Abel Meholah?
Keith Ravine
Jabbok R.
GILEAD
Joppa
Shiloh
Bethel
Gilgal
Jericho
Ramah
Jerusalem
AMMON
Moresheth
Tekoa
Gath
JUDAH
Salt Sea
Arnon R.
PHILISTIA
Besor Br.
Beersheba
Arad
MOAB
Desert of Beersheba
Kir Hareseth
Zered R.
EDOM

10,000 ft — 3050 m
5000 ft — 1525 m
2000 ft — 610 m
1000 ft — 305 m
0 (sea level) — 0 (sea level)
-1640 ft — -500 m

0 ___ 40 km.
0 ___ 40 miles

This map shows some of the key moments in Elisha's ministry.

## Elisha, the Man of God

Elisha served four different kings during his long ministry. He also ministered to ordinary people. His prayers helped supply a widow with enough oil to pay her bills. He helped a group of prophets find an ax-head that sank in the river by mistake. He advised a Shunammite woman to move away and find food before a severe famine hit the land. Elisha spent time praying and listening to God so he could help his people and his nation in their time of need.

# 1 Chronicles

The book of 1 Chronicles is a lot like 2 Samuel. Both books cover the history of Israel during the years David was king. First Chronicles, however, also has long lists of names. These names show the family trees of the twelve tribes of Israel. In particular, the family tree of King David is included. It goes all the way back to Adam and Eve. Why is this important? One reason is that these records were carefully kept for thousands of years. By the time Jesus was born, his family tree could be traced all the way back to Adam and Eve too . . . through King David!

## David's Mighty Men

Even before he became king, David's armies were made of mighty men. Thirty chiefs were famous for their strength and daring conquests. Three of them were the mightiest of all! Day after day, men came to join David's army. Tens of thousands joined his ranks. Some could use both their right and left hands to throw stones or shoot arrows from a bow. Others were experts with shields and spears. All were brave warriors prepared for battle.

## Jerusalem

King David captured Jerusalem and made it Israel's capital. He built his palace there. King David also wanted to build a temple in Jerusalem for people to come to for worship. God told David his son would build it instead. So King David made a lot of preparations for the construction of the temple, drawing up plans and gathering building supplies for his son Solomon to use.

God had plans for David and God has plans for us. Sometimes God wants us to prepare the way for people who will come after us, just as he did with David.

iStock.com/mahmutbaran

Uriah the Hittite was one of David's "Thirty," his group of famous mighty men. This sculpture shows a Hittite warrior.

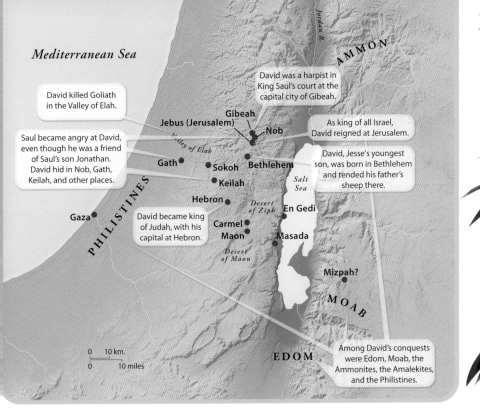

Mediterranean Sea

AMMON

Jordan R.

*David was a harpist in King Saul's court at the capital city of Gibeah.*

*David killed Goliath in the Valley of Elah.*

Gibeah

Jebus (Jerusalem)

Nob

*As king of all Israel, David reigned at Jerusalem.*

*Saul became angry at David, even though he was a friend of Saul's son Jonathan. David hid in Nob, Gath, Keilah, and other places.*

Valley of Elah

Gath

Sokoh

Bethlehem

*David, Jesse's youngest son, was born in Bethlehem and tended his father's sheep there.*

Salt Sea

Keilah

Hebron

Desert of Ziph

En Gedi

Gaza

*David became king of Judah, with his capital at Hebron.*

Carmel

Maon

Masada

PHILISTINES

Desert of Maon

Mizpah?

MOAB

0    10 km.
0        10 miles

EDOM

*Among David's conquests were Edom, Moab, the Ammonites, the Amalekites, and the Philistines.*

# Bringing the Ark to Jerusalem

The first time King David tried to bring the ark of the covenant to Jerusalem, he didn't follow God's important instructions. One of the priests died because of the wrong way they handled it. The next time, David was very careful to follow God's instructions, and it was a day of great rejoicing and celebration! They brought the ark to Jerusalem and put it in the tabernacle David had built.

© 2011 by Zondervan

The ark was designed with poles that were to be carried on the Levites' shoulders when it was moved, not on a cart pulled by oxen as King David first tried to do.

## Fun Fact!

On the day they celebrated bringing the ark to Jerusalem, everyone got a loaf of bread, a piece of meat, and a cake of raisins.

31

# 2 Chronicles

The book of 2 Chronicles follows many of the events found in 1 and 2 Kings. King Solomon built the temple in Jerusalem. After his death, only two tribes followed Solomon's son Rehoboam, and the kingdom split into two nations—Judah in the south (ruled by Rehoboam) and Israel in the north. Second Chronicles follows these events and describes the reigns of all the kings in Judah. It also gives a little bit of history on the kings who ruled over Israel. Some of Judah's kings followed God, but most didn't. It was a day of great sorrow when the Babylonian king Nebuchadnezzar destroyed the temple by fire and tore down Jerusalem's wall. But 2 Chronicles ends with a note of hope. After seventy years in captivity, King Cyrus of Persia—the newest empire to rule the land—gave the command for the Israelites to return to Jerusalem and build the temple again!

iStock.com/duncan1890

King Solomon's fame spread so wide that visitors such as the queen of Sheba came to meet him.

The inside of King Solomon's temple was overlaid with pure gold.

© Zondervan

## Key People in 2 Chronicles

Solomon

Queen of Sheba

Jehoshaphat

Jehoiada

Joash

Amaziah

Uzziah

Hezekiah

Josiah

## Role Models

Who are your role models? Who do you most want to be like? Here in 2 Chronicles, you'll find some of the most famous Bible heroes in the Old Testament. As you read about their lives and the choices they made to follow God and his ways, look for how you can use them as role models. But remember, these heroes were real people just like you. Sometimes they made mistakes and didn't choose what God said was best. We can learn from their mistakes. Read 2 Chronicles chapters 24 and 34 to learn more about Joash and Josiah, who were just kids like you when they started doing great things for God!

## Lost . . . and Found!

During this time in the history of Israel and Judah, how did the kings, priests, and people know what was right from wrong? Well, they often did whatever they wanted. One day, however, King Josiah decided to repair the temple. In the middle of the cleaning and construction, what did they find? The Bible! It wasn't the whole Bible we know today. It wasn't even called the Bible yet. It was the Book of the Law God had given Moses to share with the people. Nobody had read it for years because it had been lost! First, Shaphan the scribe read it to King Josiah. Then King Josiah gathered everyone together and read it to them. A great revival took place. And it all started by reading God's Word.

# Ezra

The book of Ezra is a testimony that God keeps his promises. The prophet Jeremiah said that God would bring the Israelites home from Babylon after seventy years of captivity. Two hundred years earlier, the prophet Isaiah said God would use a man named Cyrus to rebuild the temple. Ezra tells how both these prophesies were fulfilled. At exactly the right time, King Cyrus said the Israelites could go home and rebuild the temple.

## Meet Ezra!

Ezra was a priest who could trace his family tree all the way back to Aaron, the first high priest of Israel and Moses's brother. Ezra was also a scribe and teacher. He studied the laws God had given Moses and taught them to the people. Most of all,

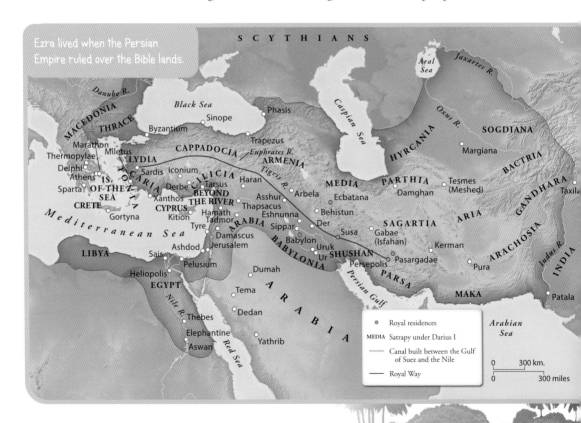

Ezra lived when the Persian Empire ruled over the Bible lands.

Ezra was a moral, godly, and honest man who trusted God and dedicated his life to serving him.

## The Journey Home

Ezra led a small group of Israelites on the long journey home from Babylon to Jerusalem. They carried valuable gold, silver, and bronze with them to give as offerings in the new temple. Who would protect them from thieves, robbers, or an ambush along the way? God! Before they set out, Ezra called for a fast. Instead of eating, everyone prayed. They asked God to keep them safe. And he did!

## Another Exodus

The return of Israelites from Babylon to Jerusalem has been called a second exodus. (The first exodus was when Moses led the Israelites out of Egypt.) As you read through the book of Ezra, compare these two important events in the history of Israel.

**EXODUS FROM EGYPT** — Pharaoh refused to let the Israelites leave.

**EXODUS BACK TO JERUSALEM** — King Cyrus invited the Israelites to leave.

Every single Israelite left Egypt in one trip.

Over 3 trips, small numbers of Israelites left for Jerusalem. Others were content to stay in Babylon.

They built the tabernacle.

They rebuilt the temple.

The generation that left Egypt rejected God's law.

A great revival took place to follow God's law.

A short distance of 529 miles took 40 years.

The long distance of 900 miles took 4 months.

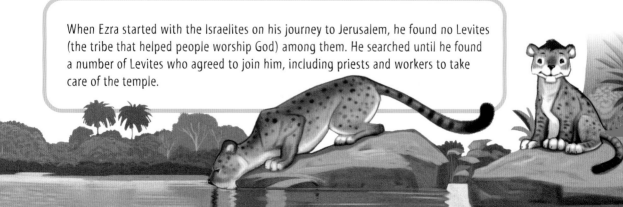

When Ezra started with the Israelites on his journey to Jerusalem, he found no Levites (the tribe that helped people worship God) among them. He searched until he found a number of Levites who agreed to join him, including priests and workers to take care of the temple.

# Nehemiah

The book of Nehemiah is a historic account of the rebuilding of Jerusalem's wall. It tells how Jerusalem's governor, Nehemiah, accomplished this task despite dangerous threats, using great leadership skills. Nehemiah was also a strong prayer warrior who trusted God to help in times of need. This book shows how God works in our lives to give us strength, courage, and skills to do important tasks for his glory.

## The City Wall

In Bible times, major cities were surrounded by a wall. Why? Walls kept wild animals out, such as lions and bears. Walls also kept enemy soldiers out. Jerusalem had been surrounded by a wall, with ten gates made of wood. When King Nebuchadnezzar came from Babylon and conquered Jerusalem, he burned down the temple and all the houses. The men in his army broke apart the wall of Jerusalem and burned its gates. The city was left in ruins.

This section of Jerusalem's ancient wall can still be seen today.

## Meet Nehemiah!

Nehemiah was one of the Israelites living as a captive in the Persian capital city of Susa. He held an important position in the Persian Empire—he was King Artaxerxes's cup-bearer. His job at the palace was to taste the food and drinks prepared for the king to test that nothing had been poisoned.

In Nehemiah's day, people didn't have their own copies of God's Word like we do now. Ezra gathered all the Israelites in Jerusalem and read the Scriptures aloud for everyone to hear.

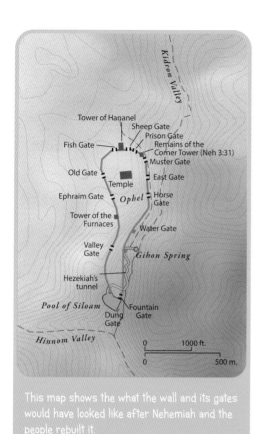

This map shows the what the wall and its gates would have looked like after Nehemiah and the people rebuilt it.

## Royal Permission

One day, Nehemiah requested the king's permission to rebuild Jerusalem's wall. King Artaxerxes then appointed Nehemiah governor of Jerusalem. The king also provided an army escort and horsemen to protect Nehemiah on his long journey back to Israel. King Artaxerxes gave Nehemiah letters to show the kings of the regions he passed through, which gave Nehemiah safe travels along the way.

## Ezra and Nehemiah

When Nehemiah arrived in Jerusalem, he had royal permission to continue rebuilding Jerusalem. This work had been started years earlier when Zerubbabel rebuilt the temple. Later, Ezra arrived to continue the work. Now Nehemiah helped Ezra. After finishing the wall, Nehemiah and Ezra worked together to bring a spiritual revival. The Israelites recommitted themselves to following God and his laws.

## Island of Elephantine

An ancient colony of Jews lived in Egypt on Elephantine Island in the Nile River. Exciting discoveries have been found there! Documents called the Elephantine papyri tell us about the same officials included in Nehemiah. Evidence like this tells us more about the historical events described in the Bible.

Olaf Tausch/CC BY 3.0

Archaeologists have discovered many ancient historic documents at this site on Elephantine Island. They help support the details found in Nehemiah.

# Esther

The book of Esther shows how God uses ordinary people to do extraordinary things. Esther was a young Jewish woman who grew up in the Persian Empire. After both of Esther's parents died, she was adopted and raised by Mordecai, one of her relatives. When she was a young woman, Xerxes, the king of Persia, chose Esther to be the new queen. Soon after, a man named Haman started a terrible plot to kill all the Jews. But due to Mordecai's guidance, Esther's courage, and God's deliverance, the Jewish people were saved. God used Esther to do mighty things . . . and he can use you too!

Public domain

This beautiful Hebrew scroll from 1750 AD contains the book of Esther.

## God's Perfect Plan

The book of Esther reminds us to put our trust in God. God is at work in our lives, even when we don't see anything happening. He is never too early. He is never too late. His plans are always perfect. As you read through the book of Esther, look for events that happened because of God's perfect plans!

## Who's Who?

Sometimes the names we read in the Bible are different than the names we read in history books. That's because names are different in different languages. For example, we know our country as the United States. But in Spanish it is called

## Important Events in Esther

**1** Mordecai saves the king's life.

**2** Haman plots to kill the Jews.

**3** Esther receives the golden scepter, which allows her to help the Jewish people.

**4** King Xerxes can't sleep and reads about what Mordecai did for him.

**5** Mordecai is honored.

**6** Haman is punished for his wicked plans.

**7** Mordecai receives the king's signet ring.

**8** Many people become Jews.

**9** Victory comes for the Jews instead of destruction.

los Estados Unidos. It's the same with names of people and places in the Bible. Shushan, the capital city of the Persian Empire, was also known as Susa. Even the queen and king had different names. Hadassah was the queen's Hebrew name, Esther was her Persian name. Ahasuerus was the king's name in Hebrew, and Xerxes was his name in Greek.

## Purim

Queen Esther's and Mordecai's actions started a brand-new Jewish holiday! It is called Purim. Every year, this holiday is celebrated to remember how God saved the Jews in Persia. Children dress up in costumes and the book of Esther is read aloud.

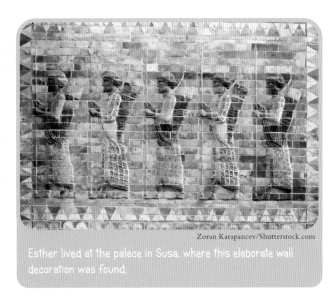

Zoran Karapancev/Shutterstock.com

Esther lived at the palace in Susa, where this elaborate wall decoration was found.

# Job

There was a man named Job who worshiped God. His life was perfect—he had a large family and enough money for thousands of livestock and many servants. But that all changed when an accuser (called "the satan" in Hebrew) asked God for permission to test Job. What happened? The accuser took away everything Job had. Job suffered, but he still kept worshiping God.

Job is a book of questions and answers. The biggest question Job and his friends asked is the same question people wrestle with today: If God is good and loving, how can he allow an innocent person to experience pain or suffering? The answer, as Job found out, is more about who God is than about pain or sorrow itself.

## Who Is God?

God is good. There is no evil in him. God is love. He is not mean or spiteful. God is wise. His wisdom is bigger and better than anything we could ever understand. Otherwise, he would not be God. God also has an eternal plan that is much bigger than what we can see. Yes, our world has pain and suffering. One day, however, God will create a new heaven and a new earth where there will be no more pain or sorrow. Right now, we may not understand our pain or the suffering in the world around us, but we can draw close to our good, loving, and wise God. Just as Job did, we can find hope and comfort in God's presence in the midst of trials. God will carry us through!

Andrzej Kubik/Shutterstock.com

## When God Speaks

God is not silent! Throughout history, he talks with us. Here are just some of the ways.

- In the very beginning of Genesis, God spoke. His words created everything in the universe.
- From inside a whirlwind, God spoke to Job about his omnipotence and power (Job 38:1).
- God spoke to the prophet Elijah in a still, small voice to whisper words of encouragement (I Kings 19:12).
- When God came to save the world, God's Word became flesh. Jesus came with the sweet, innocent voice of a tiny baby. He grew up to speak God's truths.
- God speaks to us today as we read the Bible.
- When Jesus returns to conquer evil, out of his mouth will come a sharp sword to speak judgment against Satan and sin.

ob and his friends argued back and orth, trying to give their own flawed nswers to the question of suffering. od spoke out of a powerful whirlwind tell them the true answer.

When Job lived, a person's riches were measured in the number of animals they owned. Job had seven thousand sheep, three thousand camels, five hundred yoke of oxen, and five hundred female donkeys. Plus, he had enough servants to take care of them all. He was the wealthiest person of his day!

# Psalms

Prayer, praise, thanksgiving, and worship—that's what the book of Psalms is all about. There are 150 psalms in this book, and King David wrote 73 of them. Most were sung while stringed instruments played. They are like the ancient hymns or praise songs of Bible times.

## Prayer

The psalms remind us to talk with God about *everything*! As you read through Psalms, look for reasons to pray.

## The Shepherd's Psalm

Psalm 23 is a favorite psalm. Christians memorize it. Books are written about it. It's even read at funerals. Why is it so loved? One reason is that it was written by King David, whom God called a man after his own heart. Another reason is because David was a shepherd. He knew what it was like to take care of his sheep. He also knew what it was like for God to take care of him.

## The Longest Psalm

Psalm 119 is the longest psalm. It's also the longest chapter in the Bible! It's an acrostic, which means a poem with a section written for each letter of the alphabet. (The

The lyre was a small harp that was often played when singing psalms.

Alefbet/Shutterstock.com

## Psalms for All Occasions

| Psalm 1 | Psalm 19 | Psalm 37 | Psalm 84 | Psalm 91 |
|---------|----------|----------|----------|----------|
| When you need advice | When you want to praise God | When you're worried | When you want to know God better | When you're afraid |

| Psalm 101 | Psalm 111 | Psalm 121 | Psalm 138 | Psalm 150 |
|-----------|-----------|-----------|-----------|-----------|
| When you want to do good things | When you want wisdom | When you need help | When you want to thank God for answering your prayers | When you want to worship God |

twenty-two letters in the Hebrew alphabet, that is!) Most of all, Psalm 119 praises God's Word and inspires us to love it more. It gives us examples of blessings we'll experience when we read Scripture and think about the truth of God's laws.

## A Psalm with Answers

Does God know you? Can he hear your prayers? Is he close to you or far away? Psalm 139 is a special psalm that answers many questions. Read it to find out how precious and valuable you are to God!

## Prophetic Psalms

Many New Testament writers quote verses from Psalms because the words reminded them of things that happened to Jesus. Here are some examples:

Psalm 69:9 and John 2:17
Psalm 118:26 and Matthew 21:8–9
Psalm 41:9 and Luke 22:47–48
Psalm 22:18 and John 19:23–24
Psalm 22:16 and John 20:19–29

# Proverbs

According to 1 Kings 5, King Solomon spoke three thousand proverbs. News of his great wisdom spread far and wide. Kings, queens, men, and women traveled from different nations to meet this amazing ruler anointed with wisdom by God. Many of King Solomon's proverbs are written in the book of Proverbs, alongside some written by other wise people.

## Who Is Wise?

Proverbs teaches us that if we want to really be wise, we should start with knowing God. Fools might try to be smart all on their own, but without God they can never be truly wise. That's because wisdom is who God is.

## Wise Sayings Around the World

Many cultures have collections of proverbs and wise sayings. The book of Proverbs is different from these, however, in one important way. Proverbs points people to follow God and his holy ways. We can be sure when we follow the proverbs in the Bible, we're getting the best advice!

## Hidden Treasures

Verses in Proverbs are like nuggets of gold or valuable diamonds. Here are some tips for reading this book and storing these treasures in your heart.

1. Read Proverbs slowly, one or two verses at a time.
2. Choose one proverb each morning to think about and talk with God about during the day.
3. Print out verses from Proverbs and hang them on the mirror or refrigerator to remind you of God's wise guidelines for your life.
4. Write your favorite verses on small cards to share with your family and friends.
5. Memorize key verses from Proverbs and keep them like valuable treasures in your heart.

### Did You Know?

Fragments of Proverbs were found among The Dead Sea Scrolls.

## Important Advice

According to Proverbs, it's wise to:

1. Honor God in all you do.
Proverbs 1:7

2. Respect and obey your parents.
Proverbs 1:8

3. Stay away from people who do the wrong thing.
Proverbs 1:15

4. Trust God about everything, even when you don't understand it.
Proverbs 3:5

5. Spend money, save money, and give money away in ways that honor God.
Proverbs 3:9-10

6. Accept God's discipline, because he corrects those he loves.
Proverbs 3:11

7. Be kind to other people.
Proverbs 3:27-30

8. Spread the good news of Jesus with others.
Proverbs 11:30

# Ecclesiastes

Can we be happy without God? Will lots of money make us happy? Will we be happy if we're famous and successful? Will we be happy if we get everything we want? Ecclesiastes asks these questions. Plus, it tries to answer these questions. What does this book teach us? We might be happy for a little while, but without God nothing will make us truly happy. Knowing and believing in God gives our life purpose, meaning, and contentment.

## Eternity

Forever. No beginning and no end. The Bible says God is eternal, and in Ecclesiastes we learn God put eternity in our hearts. Some people turn their backs on God and ignore eternity. They think the life they live right now on earth is the only life that matters. Ecclesiastes points out that people with this attitude can feel empty, meaningless, and hopeless. Christians do not need to feel that way. Believing in an eternal God who wants to spend wonderful days in eternity with us can give us hope and peace and joy!

King SoLomon wroTe EccLesiasTes. He had more goLd and riches Than any oTher king of IsraeL. YeT he concLuded even aLL This weaLth meanT noThing wiThouT God.

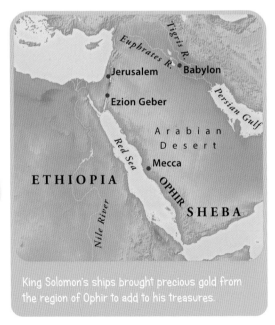

King Solomon's ships brought precious gold from the region of Ophir to add to his treasures.

## Beautiful . . . in Its Time

There are a lot of ugly things in this world. When we trust in God, however, we can be confident he will do exactly what it says in this book: he will make everything beautiful in its time, turning the ugly into good. How can he possibly do it? We can't totally understand right now. Just because we can't understand, though, doesn't mean we can't trust God will make it happen. God is so big and wise and perfect, he knows just what to do and we can trust him to do it.

While seasons in our world come and seasons go, God does not change. His love, wisdom, and goodness will always be the same. If you are going through a tough time, ask God to help you find peace in him.

## A Time for Everything

Ecclesiastes reminds us that seasons come and go, but each of them serves a purpose. What purpose might each of these times serve? Read Ecclesiastes 3:1–8 to learn more.

A time to be born.

A time to die.

A time to laugh.

A time to weep.

A time to keep.

A time to throw away.

A time to speak.

A time to be silent.

A time to love.

A time to hate.

# Song of Songs

This book is a collection of poems, or songs, that talk about the love between King Solomon and his bride. Sometimes this book is also interpreted as describing the love between God and Israel, or the love between Christ and the church. Whichever way it is read, the poems and songs inspire people to love God more and to honor marriage and the special love between a husband and a wife.

## A Student of Nature

In 1 Kings 4:29–34, we're told King Solomon was famous for his wisdom and knowledge. People came from far away to hear him speak about what he knew. He especially liked to talk about plants and animals. In this book, King Solomon mentions twenty-one different plants and fifteen different animals. Many of these examples were used to help readers picture God's love or the love between a man and a woman.

Macrovector/123RF.com

In Bible times and in some communities today, a special form of transportation called a palanquin was used to carry the bride on her wedding day.

## Weddings

A wedding was a joyful occasion and also a time to remember the way God created marriage to be. During Bible times, the bride may have worn an extravagant head covering, which was often decorated with gold coins that came from a special kind of wedding present called a dowry. Family, friends, and neighbors joined in the celebration. Musical instruments such as timbrels, tambourines, and drums provided music for dancing and rejoicing. The groom and bride could even be crowned king and queen of the event. It was tradition to feast and eat specially prepared meals together, and the wedding celebration usually lasted seven days.

## Cedars of Lebanon

Parts of this book mention the region of Lebanon. This was an area near the Mediterranean Sea and north of Solomon's kingdom that once belonged to the Phoenicians, a seafaring people known for building sturdy boats. Mountains there were covered with tall, straight cedar trees known as the cedars of Lebanon, which were famous in Bible times. King Solomon used these trees to build the temple in Jerusalem as well as palaces and other important buildings. In this book, King Solomon is compared to Lebanon and its prized cedar trees: Majestic. Strong. Important. The trees are a symbol of King Solomon as well as God, the King of kings and Lord of lords.

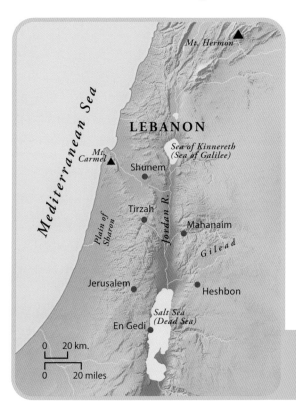

Many of the mountains, valleys, and cities named in this book (and shown on this map) were important during King Solomon's reign.

Frankincense, myrrh, and other valuable spices are mentioned in Song of Songs. Traders with great caravans of camels brought spices to Israel from faraway lands.

# Isaiah

Isaiah is the first of five books in the Old Testament known as the Major Prophets. It is named after the prophet Isaiah, who wrote it. This book has two big messages: One is God's message of warning to the Israelites about the judgment that was coming to punish their sin. The other message focuses on hope—that God will not punish the people forever, and that he will ultimately send a Savior so *everyone* can be forgiven for their sins. In Isaiah, God promises to bring his people back to him.

## Meet Isaiah

Isaiah served as prophet during the rule of four different kings of Judah: Uzziah, Jotham, Ahaz, and Hezekiah. God called Isaiah and other prophets to declare God's words to the people, give godly advice to the king, and call the children of Israel to follow God's laws.

## Politics and Power

The prophets' message was clear: Follow God and he will protect you. Turn away from God and he will use other nations to punish your sins. During Isaiah's lifetime, the Assyrian Empire was conquering all the neighboring nations and establishing their powerful rule. The northern kingdom of Israel turned away from God and fell to Assyria. When King Hezekiah and the southern kingdom of Judah listened to Isaiah's messages and followed God, God saved them from destruction in miraculous ways.

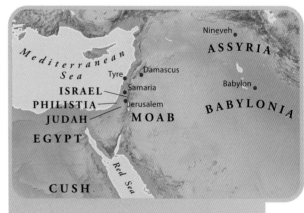

The book of Isaiah gave warnings to these cities and nations because they refused to trust in God.

This ancient scroll of the book of Isaiah was discovered in Qumran. near the Dead Sea.

## The Coming Messiah

People in New Testament times read Isaiah's prophecies and realized they pointed to Jesus, the Messiah God promised to send, because Jesus said and did things that aligned with Isaiah's words about a coming Savior. Jesus was the true fulfillment of what Isaiah prophesied! As you read through this book, pay attention to who Isaiah said the Messiah will be.

## Heaven's Throne Room

Isaiah saw the throne room of God! He viewed the Lord sitting on the throne in the heavenly temple. God's robe was so majestic and so long that its length filled the temple. Angels surrounded him, and when one of them spoke, its voice was so loud it shook the temple like an earthquake and smoke filled the room.

**Isaiah's Predictions**

**Immanuel/God with us**
Isaiah 7:14

**A great light**
Isaiah 9:2

**Prince of Peace**
Isaiah 9:6

**Servant of the Lord**
Isaiah 50:10

**Redeemer**
Isaiah 59:20

# Jeremiah

Jeremiah is an important book. In Old Testament days, Daniel read the book of Jeremiah and learned God would bring the captives in Babylon back to Jerusalem after seventy years. In New Testament days, Jesus quoted the book of Jeremiah when he drove out the people buying and selling in the temple. Today, some of the Bible's most comforting verses are found in this book for us to read when we need reassurance of God's love and care.

## The Weeping Prophet

Prophets told God's message to others. Jeremiah wrote this book so people from the kingdom of Judah would know what God needed them to know. Some of the message included the punishment God would send if the people continued their wicked ways. Jeremiah was called the weeping prophet because it made him sad to tell them about God's judgment, which could be avoided if they would just listen and follow God again. And it broke his heart to see the people of his beloved nation refuse to stop their evil ways. The book of Jeremiah, however, also includes a message of hope: One day, God would make a new covenant with his people so they could return to him.

rasoulali/Shutterstock.com

The stunning Ishtar Gate in Babylon has been rebuilt. It shows how magnificent and powerful the Babylonian Empire was during Jeremiah's lifetime.

Jeremiah warned the people of Judah that the Babylonian Empire would destroy them unless they repented and stopped doing evil. This map shows the route King Nebuchadnezzar and his armies took to conquer the land.

## A New Covenant

Why did the people need a new covenant with God? Because they had broken the first covenant they made with him to obey God's law and the Ten Commandments. In the new covenant, God said he would write his law in their minds and on their hearts. They would know him as God, and he would forgive their sins.

## God Loves Children

In Jeremiah 1:4–8, we learn God knew and loved Jeremiah even before he was born. God also said that even though Jeremiah was young, God had important things for him to do. Just like Jeremiah was special to God, you are too! God knows you. God loves you. God has an important plan for your life. He wants to talk with you about it, the way he talked with Jeremiah.

Sometimes people used pieces of broken pottery to write letters to each other. The letters on these pieces of pottery were written during some of the events that took place in the book of Jeremiah.

# Lamentations

Lamentations is a short collection of poems, or songs, written to express how sad it was when Jerusalem was destroyed. They are like sorrowful songs sung during a funeral or memorial service.

## A New World Power

About a hundred years before Lamentations was written, the Assyrian Empire had conquered the northern kingdom of Israel. Now the Babylonian Empire was rising to power. King Nebuchadnezzar and his armies conquered the Assyrian Empire. Then they marched into the southern kingdom of Judah and conquered it as well.

## Under Siege

After the Babylonian armies entered Judah, they laid siege to the city of Jerusalem for two and a half years. What is a siege? It's when an army surrounds a city and doesn't allow anyone in or out. During this time, the Babylonian army camped outside Jerusalem's city walls. Inside the city, the people ran out of water and food. When the terrible siege finally ended, the city was destroyed and its people were taken away. Only a few farmers were left to take care of the crops that would grow in the months ahead.

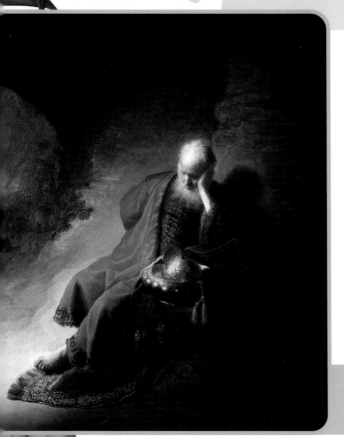

This painting depicts Jeremiah during the invasion of Jerusalem (which is shown to the left of him here).

Rembrandt van Rijn, *Jeremiah Lamenting the Destruction of Jerusalem*. Public domain.

## A Dark Day in History

It was a sad day in the Israelites' history when King Nebuchadnezzar's armies destroyed their beloved city of Jerusalem. The beautiful golden temple was burned down. The king's royal palace and every important building or home in the city was also destroyed by fire. The stone walls surrounding Jerusalem were knocked down. The city gates were burned, leaving the city open and unprotected. Worst of all, many people were killed. Others were taken far away to the city of Babylon as captives.

© 1995 Phoenix Data Systems

Archaeologists have discovered remains of the siege and destruction of Jerusalem.

## A Book of Hope

Even though Lamentations is a collection of sad songs about this horrible time in history, it is also a book of hope. It tells us the people felt sorry for sinning against God by worshiping idols, disobeying the Ten Commandments, and refusing to listen to the warnings God gave through the prophets. They realized God was punishing them for what they deserved. But they also learned of God's unfailing love for them. They trusted God would forgive their sins and were confident they would see God's goodness again. This book ends with a prayer asking God to renew them and restore them to him once again.

Many of the citizens of Jerusalem were led on a long and dangerous journey to relocate and start new lives in Babylon.

Caspian Sea

MEDIAN EMPIRE

ASSYRIA

Nineveh
Calah
Greater Zab R.
Lesser Zab R.
Ashur
Arrapkha
Ecbatana
Tigris R.
Euphrates R.
Diyala R.

Aleppo
Rezeph
Hamath

CYPRUS
Mediterranean Sea
ARAM
Arvad
Gebal (Byblos)
Riblah
Tadmor
Tyre
Damascus

NEO-
Sippar
Cuthah
Borsippa
Babylon
Nippur
Susa
ELAM

BABYLONIAN
Megiddo
Samaria
AMMON
Jerusalem
Rabbah (of the Ammonites)
Gaza
EMPIRE
Larsa
Ur
El-Arish
JUDAH
MOAB
EDOM

Memphis
Brook of Egypt
Elath
Dumah
Persian Gulf

EGYPT
Nile R.
Red Sea
Arabian Desert
Tema

Thebes

0    100 km.
0    100 miles

→ Exile from Judah

**55**

# Ezekiel

A key message in Ezekiel is, "They will know that I am the LORD." This is repeated at least twenty-five times! Each time, Ezekiel says certain events will happen that will let the people know for sure God is who he says he is. Some events are judgments, some are blessings, but they're all meant to teach people the truth: There is no other God except the God of Israel. All other gods and religions are false.

## Meet Ezekiel

Ezekiel was both a prophet and a priest. When the Babylonian king Nebuchadnezzar took ten thousand captives from Jerusalem, Ezekiel was one of them. Along with the other captives, he was forced to live far, far away in the Babylonian Empire. Ezekiel lived among the exiles there and gave God's messages to them.

## Watchman

In Bible times, a watchman had a very important job. Some watchmen kept a lookout over their flocks, making sure no wolves, lions, or bears tried to attack their animals. Other watchmen stood in a tall tower or kept guard from the city gate, and when they saw enemy armies marching their way, they would warn the city to get ready for attack. Sometimes a watchman kept an eye out for someone bringing important news to the king. God gave Ezekiel the job of being a watchman for Israel. As watchman,

Ancient historians called the Hanging Gardens of Babylon one of the seven wonders of the world. King Nebuchadnezzar designed it for his queen.

Historia/Shutterstock.com

Ezekiel was supposed to listen to God's messages and then warn the people to get ready for what God was about to do.

## Three Main Attacks

The first time King Nebuchadnezzar attacked Jerusalem, he took away the princes and educated children to make them servants in his court. This included a young man named Daniel and three of his friends. The second time Nebuchadnezzar attacked, he took away thousands of people, including Ezekiel. By this time, Daniel was starting to become a well-known official, and faithful follower of God, in the Babylonian Empire. The third time the king of Babylon attacked Jerusalem, he destroyed the city along with its temple.

Ezekiel saw important visions from God while he was next to the Chebar River with other captives.

# Attacks on Jerusalem

c. 605 BC:
First captives (including Daniel) are taken from Jerusalem to Babylon

c. 597 BC:
Second captives (including Ezekiel) are taken from Jerusalem to Babylon

c. 587 BC:
Third attack, when Jerusalem and its temple were destroyed

# Daniel

The book of Daniel has some of the most-loved stories in the Bible. These aren't just stories, though. Daniel was a real historical person who really saw God work in miraculous ways. But the book of Daniel is more than just a book about Daniel's life. The last chapters tell us about world events that would happen in the future, after Daniel died.

## Three Friends in the Fire

The story of Shadrach, Meshach, and Abednego is about more than three friends who experienced a miracle. It's a story of having faith in God no matter what happens. These three young men chose to obey God—knowing the king would punish them. They chose to believe in God—trusting he would save them from the fiery furnace. They chose to follow God's plan for their lives—hoping they'd live to tell about it.

## Ordinary, Extraordinary People

Daniel was an ordinary person who did extraordinary things for God. Even though he was captured and taken to a foreign land, he decided to keep following God, and later became an important official in the Babylonian Empire. Because of Daniel's faithfulness, King Nebuchadnezzar and King Darius both ended up praising the God Daniel trusted.

Do you want to do extraordinary things for God? Trust in God during happy times and hard times, just like Daniel. Pray to God in good times and tough times, just like Daniel. Then watch what happens. Let God take care of the rest!

Eileen Tweedy/Shutterstock.com

When King Belshazzar couldn't read the words that mysteriously appeared on the wall, Daniel was brought in to translate. Daniel told the king the words meant God was ending the sinful king's kingdom. That very night, the words came true.

# The Lions' Den

Daniel had a tough decision to make when a new law was made. If somebody prayed to anyone other than King Darius, they would be thrown into a den of lions. But Daniel knew God's law was the only law that mattered. So Daniel prayed to God, not the king, and he was thrown into the lions' den. That wasn't the end of Daniel, however. God sent an angel to protect him from the lions. When King Darius saw what happened, he made a new law that gave honor and glory to the living God!

Nastya Smirnova RF/Shutterstock.com

Balage Balogh/Archeologyillustrated.com

Archaeologists have discovered the ruins of a royal palace in Babylon. The second image shows what it may have originally looked like.

# Hosea

A key message in the book of Hosea is that God is faithful. In contrast, Hosea warned the people of Israel about their unfaithfulness to God. He explained that if the people continued to disobey God's good and holy laws, there would be consequences. At the end of Hosea's ministry, Israel received its punishment. The Assyrian armies conquered the northern kingdom of Israel and carried the Hebrews away into captivity. But that did not change God's faithfulness.

## Faithful God

What does "God is faithful" mean? For one thing, it tells us God is always faithful to his promises. God's punishment proved that when Israel disobeyed him. But God is also faithful in his perfect love for us. He was already working on his eternal plan to forgive and restore Israel to himself.

## The Northern Kingdom

Hosea's ministry was to the northern kingdom of Israel. During Hosea's life, Israel experienced wealth and prosperity. King Jeroboam II led Israel as its cities grew richer and stronger. Sadly, Israel's kings also led the people away from God by doing evil and worshiping false gods. Prophets like Hosea urged them to follow God once more.

## Marriage

The book of Hosea uses the idea of marriage to show how important love is between God and his people. God's relationship to Israel is compared to the relationship between a husband and wife. Hosea's marriage was used as an example. Even when Hosea's wife was unfaithful to him, Hosea remained faithful to her, just like when the northern kingdom of Israel was unfaithful to God, God remained faithful to them.

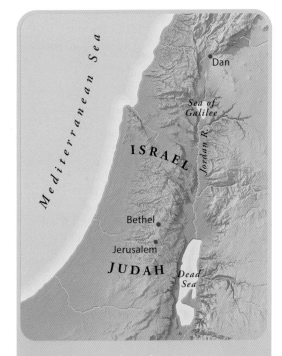

When the kingdom of Israel divided into two separate kingdoms, King Solomon's temple was in Jerusalem, inside the southern kingdom of Judah. The northern kingdom of Israel established their own religious sites and set up golden calf idols in Bethel and Dan.

## Minor Prophets

Hosea is part of a group commonly known as the minor prophets. There are twelve minor prophets, and their prophecies are also the last twelve books of the Old Testament:

| | |
|---|---|
| Hosea | Nahum |
| Joel | Habakkuk |
| Amos | Zephaniah |
| Obadiah | Haggai |
| Jonah | Zechariah |
| Micah | Malachi |

# Joel

Disaster! A cloud of locusts settled on the ground and ate everything in sight. The grain growing in the fields was wasted. The vines climbing on their poles were destroyed. Even the fruit and leaves on the fig, pomegranate, palm, and apple trees were eaten. God spoke through the prophet Joel to use this plague as an example. The day of the Lord will come with even worse disasters as judgment against evildoers. Yet a strong message of hope runs through the book of Joel. Those who turn away from their sins and turn to God will experience God's blessings.

## Locusts for Lunch?

The Bible tells of huge swarms of locusts flying like a cloud. Just imagine—millions of them! They settled on farmers' fields and gobbled up everything in sight. But did you know locusts can be eaten as food? Roasted or boiled, they are nutritious and high in protein. They can even be dried and ground into flour to use in baking. In the New Testament, John the Baptist ate locusts and honey for a healthy meal.

Alex Lerner/Shutterstock.com

Locusts are a type of grasshopper. Large swarms can number in the billions—and eat over four hundred million pounds of plants a day!

## The Character of God

Here in Joel, we learn more about who God is. Joel 2:13 says:

God is gracious.

God is compassionate and merciful.

God is slow to anger.

God shows great kindness and is abounding in love.

## The Holy Spirit

Joel prophesied that an important day was coming, when God would pour out his Spirit upon his people. This day actually took place many years later, during New Testament times, on a special holiday called Pentecost. The disciples and other followers were gathered in prayer after Jesus's death and resurrection. Suddenly the sound of a mighty wind roared into the house where they were staying. The Holy Spirit filled the believers and the new church was born. You can read more about what happened in Acts 2.

## A Special Invitation

A key part of this book is an invitation for everyone to come to God. Joel was inviting people in Judah to believe in God, and this special invitation is for you too! God loves you and wants you to get to know him better.

## Did You Know?

Locusts live on every continent across the world except Antarctica. They are usually solitary, but they'll swarm when a lot of them are gathered in one place.

# Amos

The books of Amos and Hosea have a lot in common. Both prophets were called near the beginning of King Jeroboam II's prosperous reign. Both books were written as messages for the kingdom of Israel. Both books warn God's judgment will come to Israel if they don't turn from their wicked ways. And both messages, sadly, were mostly ignored by the people.

## Meet Amos

Amos didn't get training to become a prophet. He was a farmer and a shepherd. Amos also lived in Judah. Yet God called him to be a prophet who'd give important messages to Israel. Amos obeyed God's call, left his sheep and his trees, and went north to Israel.

## The Divided Kingdom

The nation of Israel was made up of two kingdoms during Amos's lifetime. The southern kingdom was called Judah, and the northern kingdom kept the name Israel. Four other prophets—including Elijah and Elisha—had been called earlier to send messages to the northern kingdom because their leaders led them away from God. Now God wanted Amos and Hosea to warn the kingdom of Israel what would happen soon if they didn't change.

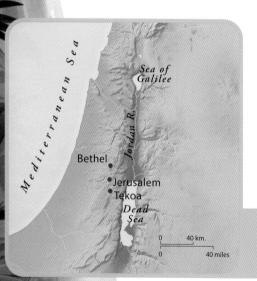

God told Amos to leave his hometown of Tekoa near Jerusalem and travel about a dozen miles north to Bethel to give God's message to Israel.

The sycamore-fig is a large tree prized for its shade and its fruit.

valenzi/123RF.com

## The Sycamore-Fig Tree

As a farmer, Amos raised fruit from the sycamore-fig tree. This tree was common in Israel: King David employed farmers to tend to his crop, and in the New Testament, Zacchaeus climbed one to watch Jesus enter the town of Jericho.

## Creator God

In his message to Israel, Amos challenged the people to worship their Creator. Amos spoke as a farmer to a group of people whose lives depended on their fields and flocks—and who were turning to idols to ask for rain and good crops. God's message to them? Who makes the day change to night and the night into morning? Who formed the mountains and walks among the clouds? Who calls for the water and sends rain on the earth? Not an idol. Not anything in the earth. The Lord God Almighty is his name!

# Obadiah

Jerusalem was under attack! Would their neighbors, the nation of Edom, help them? No! The Edomites stood by and watched the destruction. Some laughed at Jerusalem's sadness and troubles. Other Edomites even helped Jerusalem's enemies! Because of this, God announced he would punish Edom.

This is an important message to us today. The people in Jerusalem were God's chosen people, and he still loved them. Obadiah tells us God punishes those who hurt his people or do not help in their time of need.

## Follow the Leader!

What matters to God? How we treat other people. As you read through Obadiah, look for these guidelines on how to act toward others:

1. Volunteer to help in times of need.

2. Let your actions be those of a friend.

3. Don't rejoice when others suffer.

4. Be strong for others when they are weak.

5. Protect what belongs to others.

Vadim Petrakov/Shutterstock.com

This is an ancient copper mine in Timna National Park, which was part of Edom during Bible times.

## Relatives

Edom wasn't just Jerusalem's neighbor; they were relatives! Genesis 36 tells us about the Edomites, whose ancestor was Esau. Esau and Jacob were twin brothers, and Jacob was the ancestor of the Jews. These twins, however, didn't get along. All through history, their descendants were enemies. This continued on to the New Testament with Herod the Great, who was a descendant of the Edomites.[1] Herod tried to kill Jesus, the King of the Jews.

## Faith Founded on Fact

For a long time, historians and archaeologists couldn't find evidence of how the Edomites lived . . . until an ancient copper mine was discovered in Timna National Park, which is in an area that was once part of Edom. These findings show us that what the Bible tells us about Edom aligns with historical fact!

## Prophecy Fulfilled

The prophet Obadiah announced Edom's punishment because they invaded Judah and plundered Jerusalem. This prophecy came true in 325 BC, when Edom was conquered by an Arab tribe called the Nabateans. They established their capital in Petra. An impressive fortress, tombs, and temples were carved into the cliffs. Today, Petra is one of the most famous historic sites in the world.[2]

Impressive buildings like this were carved into Petra's rocks.

William D. Mounce

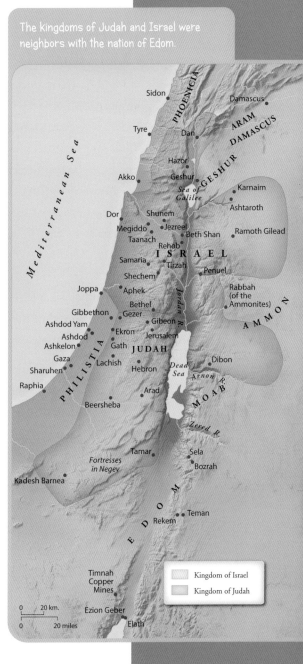

The kingdoms of Judah and Israel were neighbors with the nation of Edom.

Sidon
PHOENICIA
Damascus
Tyre
ARAM DAMASCUS
Dan
Hazor
Akko
Geshur
GESHUR
Sea of Galilee
Karnaim
Ashtaroth
Dor
Shunem
Megiddo
Jezreel
Beth Shan
Ramoth Gilead
Taanach
Rehob
ISRAEL
Samaria
Tirzah
Shechem
Penuel
Joppa
Aphek
Rabbah (of the Ammonites)
Bethel
AMMON
Gibbethon
Gezer
Ashdod Yam
Gibeon
Ashdod
Ekron
Jerusalem
Ashkelon
Gath
JUDAH
Gaza
Dibon
Sharuhen
Lachish
Hebron
Dead Sea
Arnon R.
Raphia
PHILISTIA
Arad
MOAB
Beersheba
Zered R.
Tamar
Sela
Fortresses in Negev
Bozrah
Kadesh Barnea
EDOM
Teman
Rekem

Mediterranean Sea
Jordan R.

| | Kingdom of Israel |
| | Kingdom of Judah |

Timnah Copper Mines

0   20 km.
0   20 miles

Ezion Geber
Elath

# Jonah

The book of Jonah is a love story. It's about God's great love for all people. Yes, God loves his chosen people, the Hebrew children. The Old Testament is full of those examples. Jonah, however, shows us that God loves every person!

When God saw how wicked the people in Nineveh were, he sent the prophet Jonah to warn them he was going to punish them for their evil. God announced he would destroy Nineveh in forty days. Why did God give them a forty-day warning? Why did God send prophets to other people with warnings? The Bible says God doesn't want anyone to die. Of course he doesn't. He loves us!

## A Happy Ending

The book of Jonah has a happy ending. When the people in Nineveh heard Jonah's message, they all repented of their sins and stopped doing evil. They fasted instead and prayed to God with their whole hearts. They believed in God. And in his great love for them, God saw their response and decided not to destroy Nineveh after all. So while the book of Jonah is a love story, it's also about one of the greatest revivals ever to happen in the history of the world.

## Anywhere and Everywhere

Jonah didn't want to go to Nineveh at first and had to pray for forgiveness when he tried to disobey God. Where did Jonah pray? From inside a huge fish! And God heard him. This shows we can pray anywhere. Where do you like to pray? Do you say good morning to God in bed

For many years, Nineveh was the capital city of Assyria—a major enemy of Israel and Judah. This shows what Nineveh may have looked like.

Balage Balogh/Archaeologyillustrated.com

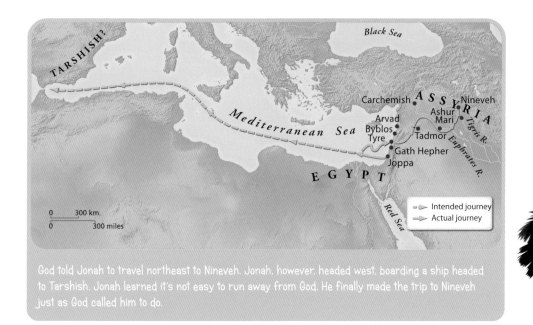

God told Jonah to travel northeast to Nineveh. Jonah, however, headed west, boarding a ship headed to Tarshish. Jonah learned it's not easy to run away from God. He finally made the trip to Nineveh just as God called him to do.

when you wake up? Do you fold your hands at the table and thank him for your food? No matter when or where, God wants to hear from you. And because God is right there with you, he can always hear because he's everywhere you are. Just like he was with Jonah.

Zev Radovan/
www.biblelandpictures.com

This is a model of a Canaanite 'Tarshish' merchant ship, a typical sailing vessel in Jonah's day.

## Jesus and Jonah

Jesus referred to Jonah's experience inside the fish as an example of his own upcoming death and resurrection. Jesus also suggested his listeners should respond to his message of repentance even more than the people of Nineveh responded to Jonah's. Why? Because someone greater than Jonah was here. That someone was Jesus, the actual Son of God.

# Micah

Just like the prophet Amos, Micah was from the countryside. Yet God called Micah to give a message to two very important cities: Samaria, the capital city of the northern kingdom of Israel; and Jerusalem, the capital city of the southern kingdom of Judah. God's main message was a cry for justice. Stop robbing and stealing. Stop planning wrong things. Stop worshiping idols. Instead, act with justice. Show mercy to others. Walk humbly with your God. These are still important messages for believers today. But Micah also made a significant prophesy as well.

## The Star Verse of the Old Testament

This book has one of the most important verses in the entire Old Testament. Micah 5:2 says the coming Messiah will be born in Bethlehem. About seven hundred years later, it happened just as God said it would. Caesar Augustus decreed everyone had to be counted in a census. Since they were descendants of King David, Joseph and Mary were commanded to leave their small village and go to David's hometown of Bethlehem to be counted. When they arrived, Jesus was born—right where the prophet Micah said he would be!

Micah warns judgment will come to the Hebrew nations because of their sins. It came in the form of conquest. The writing on this stone tablet describes how the Assyrian armies attacked the nations in that region, including Israel.

Alpha Stock/Alamy Stock Photo

## Little Town of Bethlehem

There's a lot of history in Bethlehem! It was an important town in Old Testament times. Ruth moved here with her mother-in-law, Naomi, where she later married Boaz and raised their family. Their great-grandson King David was born in Bethlehem. Before he was king, David was a shepherd, watching his father's flocks of sheep in the hills surrounding the town. In the New Testament, Bethlehem takes on new importance when Jesus is born. On that special night, shepherds were watching their flocks on those same hills. Suddenly, a glorious host (crowd) of angels appeared among the stars in the night sky, announcing a new King had been born.

## No Fishing!

Micah ends with one of the most hope-filled truths in the Bible: that God is in the business of forgiving sins. He is willing to forgive our sins when we ask for forgiveness. He even promises to forget the sins he forgives us for. He will throw them to the bottom of the ocean where nobody can ever find them again. It's like there's a permanent No Fishing sign posted over that spot.

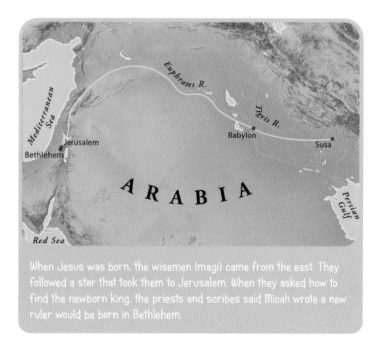

When Jesus was born, the wisemen (magi) came from the east. They followed a star that took them to Jerusalem. When they asked how to find the newborn king, the priests and scribes said Micah wrote a new ruler would be born in Bethlehem.

# Nahum

The short book of Nahum is divided into three main parts. The first part praises the goodness of God. The second part reassures Judah that God will protect them from the cruel nation of Assyria. The third part warns Assyria that their capital city of Nineveh will be destroyed because of their evil deeds against other nations.

## Nahum and Jonah

One hundred years before Nahum's prophecy, Jonah also had a special message, this one directly for Nineveh, the capital city of Assyria. When Jonah told the people God's warning that they would be punished for their evil acts, the king and everyone in the city responded by repenting, and so God didn't destroy the city after all. However, Nahum's prophecy shows us they didn't turn away from their wicked ways for good. Nahum's words to Judah warned that Nineveh would now be punished because of their sins . . . and it was.

Chariots were a symbol of strength in battle. Nahum prophesied that the Assyrians' chariots would be destroyed because of the destruction they caused wherever they went.

## The Rise and Fall of Nations

When you read history books or encyclopedias, they tell of the rise and fall of different nations—the key dates the empire came to power and when it was destroyed, as well as who the kings were and their military strategies. In the book of Nahum, however, the prophet Nahum makes it very clear. God is in control of the nations, and he blesses the nations who follow him and his ways. He punishes wicked nations who do not.

## God Is Good

How could Nahum's message be about how good God is if God allowed a city to be destroyed? Things like this can be hard to understand, usually because we try to figure out God based on what people are like. But God is not a big person. When he's angry, it's not like our anger—it's perfect anger. When he is loving, it's not like our love—it's perfect love. When he punishes evil, it's not how we would punish someone—it's perfect punishment. The book of Nahum says God is slow to anger and always good. He is a place of safety for those in trouble. He takes care of everyone who trusts in him.

In this book, the Assyrians are compared to lions who hunt and kill their prey—because the Assyrians were very cruel. Nahum reassured Judah that God is different than the Assyrians. He is slow to anger but mighty in power and would not leave the guilty unpunished.

Between Jonah's message and Nahum's prophecy, a lot had changed in Ninevah:

- It had become the most renown city in the world because of its beauty and cultural importance.
- Tall walls of almost 100 feet had been build around the city to protect it.
- Many people believed that Ninevah was so powerful and safe, it would never be destroyed.

So the inhabitants must have been very surprised when God sent armies and floods that broke down their walls and destroyed everything! In fact, almost nothing remains of this once-great city.

# Habakkuk

Sometimes people struggle with their faith in God and they want to know "Why?" This book is about a prophet named Habakkuk who questioned God and wondered why he didn't immediately punish evildoers. After God gave him an answer, Habakkuk had another question, this one asking why God would use an eviler nation—Babylon—to punish Judah. By the end of the book, Habakkuk made an important decision. He chose to believe in God and trust him . . . no matter what happened!

## Trust Is a Choice

Habakkuk feared the upcoming Babylonian invasion might destroy everything in Judah—such as the fig trees, the grapevines, and the olive trees, as well as the sheep and goats. Because people's food and money came from their crops and animals, this would be a difficult time. By the end of this book, however, Habakkuk chose to trust God would take care of his people.

## Shadrach, Meshach, Abednego . . . and Habakkuk?

In the book of Daniel, we learn about three friends who refused to worship King Nebuchadnezzar's giant statue and were ordered to be thrown into the fiery furnace. They knew God could save them from their punishment, but whether or not he did, they chose to trust in him. Just like Habakkuk did. Read Habakkuk 3:17–18 and Daniel 3:17–18 to learn more.

Habakkuk compared The Babylonian Empire To a fisherman and his net. They were going To gather up all The nations To destroy Them.

## Big Questions

Habakkuk had questions about God. Big questions. So he talked with God about them, then waited and listened for God to speak to him. Do you have questions about God? Talk with him about them just like Habakkuk did. Then wait and listen for God to speak to you. Read your Bible while you wait. When God speaks, it always lines up with the Bible. That's the truth!

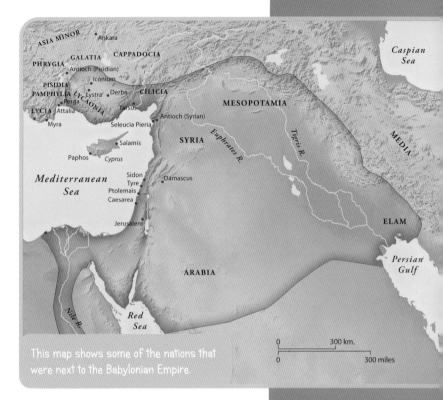

This map shows some of the nations that were next to the Babylonian Empire.

## Pray for Our Nation

Many people gather in their cities, schools, and churches to pray for America on the National Day of Prayer. Habakkuk prayed for his nation too. He saw the violence, trouble, and arguing among Judah's leaders. He saw people didn't obey the laws and justice was not done. Just as Habakkuk prayed for his people, we can pray for our people. And just as Habakkuk trusted God to work out his perfect plan in Old Testament times, we can trust God to work out his perfect plan today.

The book of Habakkuk closes with a hymn singing praises to the God who saves and cares for us. It was to be sung while stringed instruments played.

# Zephaniah

Have you ever thought it isn't fair when someone hurts you or somebody you know? Have you ever wondered how mean, angry people can get their own way? Have you ever been confused when evil laws are voted in and wrong things are allowed to happen? The book of Zephaniah is a promise from God that he will take care of all the evil everywhere—at exactly the best time.

## Punishment or Blessing?

Zephaniah talks about a future event when God will punish evil once and for all. But this book also talks about how God punishes some evil right away. Zephaniah warned different nations and cities that God would punish them if they continued to do evil. The good news? Some people listened to the prophet's warning and changed their ways.

## Revival!

King Amon had worshiped idols, not God, and led all of Judah into sin. Then his son Josiah became the king. At that time, God spoke through Zephaniah to warn Judah and its capital city of Jerusalem to turn from their wicked and shameful ways and to worship God instead. What happened next is one of the most wonderful events in Bible history! The Book of the Law (which was possibly the book of Deuteronomy and contained God's laws) was found in the temple after being lost for many years. King Josiah then read it for the very first time. It changed his life forever! He led Judah in a great revival where they repented of their many sins and followed God, just as Zephaniah had urged them to do.

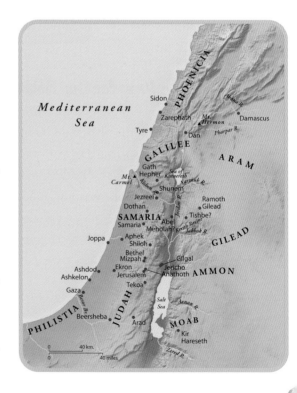

## Family Tree

The prophet Zephaniah and King Josiah were distant cousins through the family tree of King Hezekiah, one of Judah's most God-honoring rulers. Hezekiah was Zephaniah's great-great grandfather and Josiah's great grandfather!

## God Rejoices

The message at the end of Zephaniah is one of great hope and rejoicing. We can sing with joy because God loves us so much! We can be glad with our whole heart because God has an amazing plan for us. God delights in us and rejoices over us too. Just imagine! God sings songs of great joy because of his wonderful love for us. He is with us and is mighty to save!

Many Bible scholars think Zephaniah's warning to Judah came before King Josiah ordered the temple to be repaired. The Book of the Law was found during that construction project.

## Zephaniah's Family Tree

Hezekiah

Amariah → Manasseh

Gedaliah → Amon

Cushi → Josiah

Zephaniah

# Haggai

A key message in the book of Haggai is about time. After the captives returned to Jerusalem, they were so busy taking care of their own business that they didn't have time to take care of God's. Haggai's message encouraged them to get their priorities straight and put God first. That meant taking time to rebuild the temple. After that, they could spend time with their other projects and God would bless them.

## The History Behind Haggai

Haggai was written when Darius was king of the Persian Empire. Darius gave the Hebrews permission to continue rebuilding the temple that had been destroyed years ago by the Babylonian Empire. Some of the first captives who returned to Jerusalem had started to work on the temple years earlier, and they'd built a new altar and laid the temple's foundation. The problem was, people then began spending so much time building their own houses and barns that they didn't have time to finish the temple. God sent a message through Haggai to Zerubbabel, Judah's governor, and Joshua, the high priest. It was time to finish the work!

© 2018 by Zondervan

The second temple is also known as Zerubbabel's Temple. This model of Jerusalem shows where it was probably located (center).

## Watch Your Time

As you read through Haggai, look for these guidelines on how to spend your time.

1. Think carefully about what you do with your time.

2. God cares about how you spend your time.

3. Ask God to show you what he wants you to do.

4. Be strong, and work at what God wants you to do.

5. God is with you while you work.

6. Don't fear that God's task is too hard to do.

7. Ask the Holy Spirit to give you strength.

8. Look for God's blessings when you put him first.

One of the first things the returning exiles did was rebuild the temple's altar. They offered prayers and sacrifices on the altar even before the rest of the temple was built.

joshimerbin/Shutterstock.com

## It's About Time

How do we spend our time? The book of Haggai encourages us to think about it. Do we spend time doing things that show we put God first in our heart? Or are we so busy doing our own things that we forget to do what God wants us to do? Haggai's message shows that it's easy to do things that can be a waste of our time. When we put God first, we experience success with everything else we do.

# Zechariah

What is a vision? It's like a movie—but it all happens inside someone's head, and it's about the future. This book is about messages and visions God gave the prophet Zechariah. He wanted Zechariah to encourage the people to finish rebuilding the temple. Like the prophet Haggai, Zechariah was sent to preach to the exiles who had returned from captivity in Babylon. The message in both Haggai and Zechariah was the same: God is with you. He will help you finish the job you started.

## God's Spirit

Zechariah's message is encouraging. The Hebrews didn't need to trust in their own strength to rebuild the temple. They didn't need their own power to help with their construction project. God said he would meet all their needs as they worked, through the presence of his Spirit (see Zechariah 4:6).

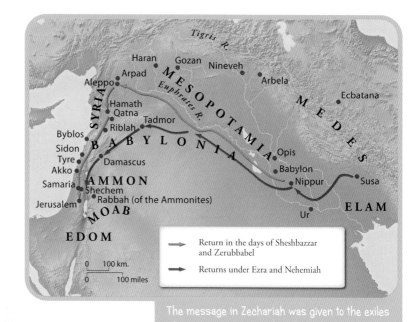

The message in Zechariah was given to the exiles who returned to Jerusalem from their captivity.

80

## The Coming Messiah

Zechariah is the next-to-last book in the Old Testament. It's in a great place because this book contains many messages about the coming Messiah. As you read, look for these prophecies that were fulfilled in the New Testament through the life and death of Jesus Christ.

- Triumphal entry into Jerusalem on a donkey (Zechariah 9:9 and John 12:14–15)
- The arrest of the Messiah (Zechariah 13:7 and Matthew 26:54–56)
- The disciples scattering in fear (Zechariah 13:7 and Mark 14:27)
- Thirty pieces of silver thrown to the potter's field (Zechariah 11:12–13 and Matthew 27:9–10)
- His side will be pierced (Zechariah 12:10 and John 19:37)

### Fun Fact

Can you whistle? God can! In this book, God says he will whistle to people and call them to him. When they come, he will bless them! See Zechariah 10:7–8.

## An Important Feast

The book of Zechariah says a day is coming when everyone will go to Jerusalem every year to celebrate the Feast of Tabernacles. This holiday is also called Sukkot or Festival of Booths. Many people celebrate this festival today by building small booths (huts) outside their home and decorating them with branches from palm trees or olive trees. This feast celebrates the fall harvest. It's also a time to remember the years the Israelites wandered in the wilderness and God provided for all their needs.

ChameleonsEye/Shutterstock.com

This is an example of a sukkah, a temporary hut the Jewish people put up for the Feast of Tabernacles.

# Malachi

This is the last book of the Minor Prophets and the last book in the Old Testament. One of the messages Malachi gives from God says a messenger will come to "prepare the way before me." In Matthew, the first book of the New Testament and the next book in the Bible, we learn who this person is: John the Baptist. John prepared the way for Jesus, the Messiah, by calling people to repent and turn away from their sins.

## Forever the Same

"I do not change," God says in Malachi. This is a very important part of who God is. God loved the people of Israel, and he loves you. In Bible times, God forgave people who were sorry for their sins. Today, he'll forgive you. God is the same yesterday, today, and tomorrow. His plans and promises are still as important today as they were in the days the Bible was written. You can count on it, because God never changes.

### Did You Know?

Bible scholars think the book of Malachi was written around 450 BC. Isn't God amazing? More than four centuries before John the Baptist's birth, God told Malachi something that the Gospel writers saw as proof God was preparing the way for Jesus!

## Giving Our Best

An important message in Malachi is that we should give our best to God. In Malachi's time, people brought their best crops, lamb, or goat to offer as burnt sacrifices on the altar. Today, we don't put a sheep or a bowl of olives in the offering basket at church. But we can still offer our best when we worship God.

### Ways to Honor God

Carefully consider your words and choices.

Read the Bible every day.

Before you spend any money you get, give part of it in the offering at church.

Be honest and tell the truth.

Share the good news about Jesus with others.

© 2011 by Zondervan

The incense altar was a place for the Hebrew priests to burn incense as an offering. We can present offerings to worship God today by honoring him with our time, talents, money, and the choices we make.

## Return to God

In Malachi, God calls his children to come back to him. God promises that if we return to him, he will return to us. He is the God of second chances. Do you know someone who has walked away from God? Invite them to come back to him. God will welcome them with open arms.

# Matthew

People in Bible times didn't like tax collectors. They often made people pay extra money so they could get rich. The Jews especially didn't like when other Jews were tax collectors, because tax collectors worked for the Roman Empire, who'd conquered the Jews and ruled over their people. So did anybody like Matthew, a Jewish tax collector? Jesus did! To everyone's surprise, Jesus called Matthew to follow him. Matthew left his tax booth, became a disciple, and ended up writing this book. He wanted to tell the Jewish people that their promised Messiah had come at last!

## Treasures to Keep

Matthew had a lot to say about money. This was probably because his job was in finance. He recorded Jesus's godly advice on how to handle your money—included in the illustration to the right.

holylandphotos.org

Matthew's tax booth was probably located along this road leading to the Mount of Beatitudes. This is the hill where Matthew recorded Jesus sitting down to teach the Beatitudes in his Sermon on the Mount.

This coin, with the image of Julius Caesar, may have been like the one the Pharisees showed Jesus when they asked him if they should pay their taxes to Caesar.

Todd Bolen/
BiblePlaces.com

## A Party with Jesus

After he became a disciple, one of the first things Matthew did was host a party! Tax collectors and sinners came. In fact, Jesus became known as the friend of tax collectors and sinners (see Matthew 11:19). When asked why he was their friend, Jesus said he came to earth for the sinners, not the people who had already been saved. (Read about it in Matthew 9:9–13.)

# Eyewitness Report

In court, an eyewitness's testimony is very valuable. Why? Because they saw what happened. Matthew followed Jesus and was an eyewitness to many events in this book. This is one of the reasons we can be sure Jesus is God and is the Savior of the world. If Matthew saw and believed, we can believe too!

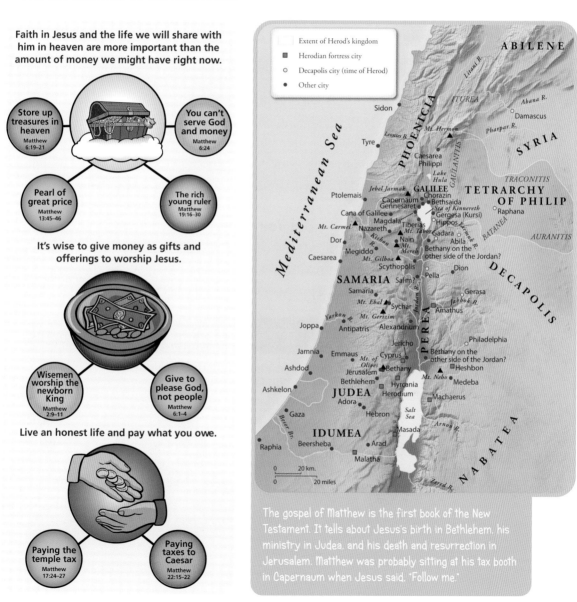

**Faith in Jesus and the life we will share with him in heaven are more important than the amount of money we might have right now.**

Store up treasures in heaven
Matthew 6:19–21

You can't serve God and money
Matthew 6:24

Pearl of great price
Matthew 13:45–46

The rich young ruler
Matthew 19:16–30

**It's wise to give money as gifts and offerings to worship Jesus.**

Wisemen worship the newborn King
Matthew 2:9–11

Give to please God, not people
Matthew 6:1–4

**Live an honest life and pay what you owe.**

Paying the temple tax
Matthew 17:24–27

Paying taxes to Caesar
Matthew 22:15–22

Extent of Herod's kingdom
Herodian fortress city
Decapolis city (time of Herod)
Other city

The gospel of Matthew is the first book of the New Testament. It tells about Jesus's birth in Bethlehem, his ministry in Judea, and his death and resurrection in Jerusalem. Matthew was probably sitting at his tax booth in Capernaum when Jesus said, "Follow me."

# Mark

The gospel of Mark focuses on the last few years of Jesus's life. It opens with Jesus's baptism in the Jordan River and his preparation for ministry. It then shows the miracles and teaching Jesus did in cities around the Sea of Galilee. Both these sections give evidence that prove Jesus was not an ordinary man or just an important teacher. Mark wanted his readers to know Jesus is the Son of God, the promised Messiah.

## A Suffering Servant

This book also shows Jesus as a servant, obeying God's plan to offer himself as a sacrifice for our sins. Mark follows Jesus on his journey to Jerusalem where he suffered, died on the cross, and came to life again. Mark's message? Christians should be willing to suffer for Christ and live the new life he promises to those who believe in him.

## Did You Know?

According to the book of Acts, Mark—whose Hebrew name was John—went on a missionary trip with Paul and Barnabas. Unfortunately, Mark deserted the trip and went back home to Jerusalem. This caused people to be mad at him for a while. The

### Mark—The Gospel of the Servant-Messiah

Mark provides details of Jesus's ministry, including his death on the cross and resurrection from the dead.

| John the Baptist prepares people for the Messiah (1:1-13) | Jesus's ministry (1:1—8:30) | Peter says Jesus is the Messiah and Jesus first predicts his death (8:27-38) | Jesus enters Jerusalem, dies, and is resurrected (11-16) |

Bible doesn't explain what happened on that trip, but later Mark went on another missionary journey with Barnabas. He helped Peter in Rome, probably putting together the gospel of Mark from many of Peter's teachings. Mark even became a friend to Paul, helping with his ministry. Mark's story reminds us that God is a God of second chances. He can use all of us, even when we make mistakes.

## Miracle Maker

Mark wrote this book to the believers in Rome, especially the Gentiles (non-Jewish people) who had become Christians. He described the many miracles Jesus performed as proof that Jesus is God.

## The First Gospel

Many Bible scholars think that Mark was the first of the four gospels to be written. There are many events in Mark that are also included in the books of Matthew and Luke, hinting Matthew and Luke may have referenced Mark's writings and other sources when writing their own gospels.

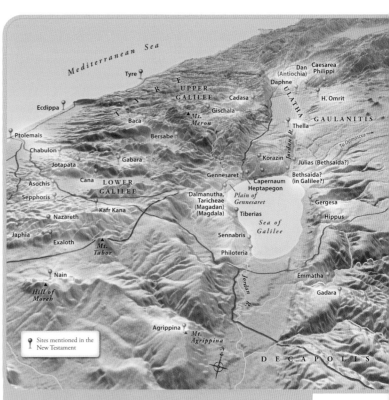

Mark includes details of the ministry Jesus did in villages and cities around the Sea of Galilee.

Only one miracle is recorded in all four gospels: when Jesus fed five thousand people with only five loaves of bread and two fish. Everyone was overcome with amazement!

# Luke

In the first part of this book, Luke introduces us to Jesus—his genealogy, the miraculous events leading up to his birth, the wonderful night he was born, and small glimpses into his boyhood. In the second part, we learn about Jesus's ministry, mostly around the region of Galilee. The third part follows Jesus on his journey toward Jerusalem. In the final part of this book, we learn what happened when Jesus was arrested, died on the cross, came to life again, met with his followers, and was taken up into heaven. Luke wanted to show how Jesus is a real, historical person, the Son of God who died on the cross to bring salvation to the world.

## Merry Christmas!

The second chapter of Luke is everyone's favorite Christmas story! It's read aloud at church services, at Christmas plays, and by families celebrating together on Christmas morning. But it's more than a story. Those who believe in its wonderful message know it's the most important event that ever happened in the history of the world.

**Women in Luke**

Elizabeth

Mary

Anna

Widow of Nain

Woman who was healed by Jesus

Women who ministered to Jesus

Martha and Mary

Woman with two coins

Women at the tomb

Psephinus Tower
Tyropoeon Street
Present Damascus Gate
Bridge Over Valley ("Wilson's Arch")
Xystus (Greek exercise hall)
Hasmonean Palace
Traditional Crucifixion Site
Herod's Towers
Herod's Royal Palace
Mt. Zion ("Upper City")
Theater
Traditional Upper Room?
Essene Gate
House of Caiaphas
Ashpot Gate (Tekoa Gate)
HINNOM VALLEY
N
Maximum city growth within walls by AD 70
Hippodrome
"Garden Tomb" (alternate crucifixion site)
Antonia Fortress (later Praetorium?)
Bezetha ("New City")
Pool of Bethesda
Temple
Gentiles Court
Huldah Gates and Stairways
Gihon Spring
City of David ("Lower City")
Pool of Siloam
MOUNT OF OLIVES
KIDRON VALLEY

This is the city of Jerusalem as Jesus knew it.

Luke is the only author who documented an important event that happened when Jesus was twelve. Jesus visited Jerusalem for Passover with his parents, Mary and Joseph. When his parents left, they realized Jesus wasn't with them. They finally found him at the temple with the teachers, listening and asking questions. Everyone was amazed at Jesus's understanding and answers.

## Fun Fact

Everyone is important to Jesus, even when the world doesn't think they are. In Luke's time, women were often overlooked, but the gospel of Luke records how Jesus showed compassion to many different women. Plus, there were important women in Jesus's life. Who are some of these women Luke wants us to meet?

## Bible Detectives

Luke, the author of this book, was a doctor. But he became a type of detective when he decided to write this gospel. This book is filled

Albrecht Dürer, *Christ Among the Doctors*. Artefact/Alamy Stock Photo

with eyewitness accounts. Luke wasn't there during Jesus's ministry, so he likely interviewed people to get the facts, feelings, and behind-the-scene details. Even today, there are Bible detectives who follow in Luke's footsteps. They search for clues to the history, science, and archaeology behind the people and events of Bible times. Maybe one day you'd like to join them in their exciting adventures!

# John

John is the fourth book about Jesus's life. Today, these first four books in the New Testament are called the Gospels. This gospel was written by John, who was a close friend of Jesus. Inside its pages, we see that the creator of the universe, the living and eternal Word (God), cares about each one of us. John wrote

John stood at the foot of the cross. He made sure to tell us that Jesus went to the cross for a purpose: Old Testament Scriptures were fulfilled. The penalty for sin was paid. The judgment of God was satisfied. And because of that, the free gift of salvation is now offered to anyone and everyone who believes.

this book so we can choose to believe Jesus is the Christ, and by believing be able to live with him forever after we die. But not only does Jesus want us to know him as our Lord and Savior, he also wants us to know him as our closest friend. Just like John.

## The Great *I AM*

In Exodus, God told Moses his name is *I AM*. As you read through John, look for the seven times Jesus said, "I am." Jesus wasn't just talking—he was telling everyone who was listening that he is God. He existed before the beginning of time. He was there at creation, and everything was made by him. He was there talking with Moses and there through all the events in the Old Testament. He was born as a baby and grew up to be the Savior of the world. He is here with you right now. He wants to live with you forever. He was. He is. He will always be. He's the great *I AM*!

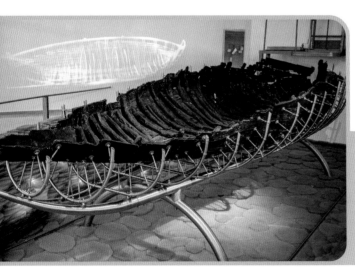

John and some of the other disciples were fishermen. This 2,000-year-old fishing boat, nicknamed the "Jesus boat," was found in the mud along the shores of the Sea of Galilee. It is similar to the boats John and the disciples would have sailed in during their time with Jesus.

Logan Bush/Shutterstock.com

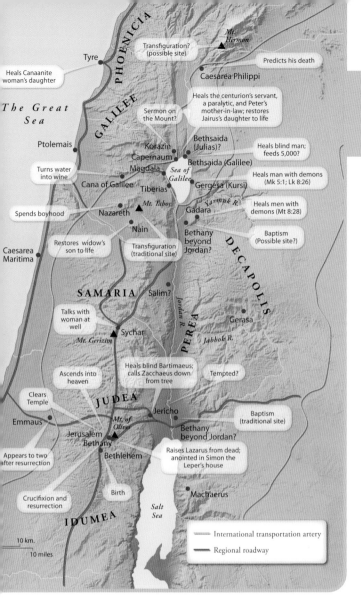

PHOENICIA

Tyre

Transfiguration?
(possible site)

Mt.
Hermon

Predicts his death

Heals Canaanite
woman's daughter

Caesarea Philippi

GALILEE

The Great
Sea

Sermon on
the Mount?

Heals the centurion's servant,
a paralytic, and Peter's
mother-in-law; restores
Jairus's daughter to life

Ptolemais

Korazin

Capernaum

Bethsaida
(Julias)?

Heals blind man;
feeds 5,000?

Magdala

Sea of
Galilee

Bethsaida (Galilee)

Turns water
into wine

Cana of Galilee

Tiberias

Gergesa (Kursi)

Heals man with demons
(Mk 5:1; Lk 8:26)

Mt. Tabor

Yarmuk R.

Spends boyhood

Nazareth

Gadara

Heals men with
demons (Mt 8:28)

Nain

Restores widow's
son to life

Transfiguration
(traditional site)

Bethany
beyond
Jordan?

DECAPOLIS

Baptism
(Possible site?)

Caesarea
Maritima

SAMARIA

Salim?

Talks with
woman at
well

Gerasa

Mt. Gerizim

Sychar

PEREA

Jordan R.

Jabbok R.

Ascends into
heaven

Heals blind Bartimaeus;
calls Zacchaeus down
from tree

Tempted?

Clears
Temple

JUDEA

Emmaus

Jericho

Mt. of
Olives

Baptism
(traditional site)

Jerusalem
Bethany

Bethany
beyond Jordan?

Appears to two
after resurrection

Bethlehem

Raises Lazarus from dead;
anointed in Simon the
Leper's house

Crucifixion and
resurrection

Birth

Machaerus

IDUMEA

Salt
Sea

10 km.

10 miles

International transportation artery

Regional roadway

In John, we learn about Jesus's
miracles and ministry, which prove
Jesus is God and not just an important
teacher.

Public domain

Parts of John 18 and 19 are on this
ancient fragment of papyrus. It is
one of the oldest pieces of the New
Testament ever found—written in
the second century AD.

## The Holy Spirit

In John, we learn all about the Holy Spirit from Jesus's teachings. Who is the Holy Spirit?
He is our advocate and helper. He comforts us when we are sad or lonely. He helps us rec-
ognize our sins. He teaches us and guides us toward the truth. The Holy Spirit promises
to live inside everyone who believes in Jesus.

# Acts

Luke wrote the books of Luke and Acts because he wanted us to be certain that Jesus told the truth and was a real person. The book of Luke tells us about Jesus's life and his ministry. In Acts, Jesus's ministry continues through the work of believers, due to the power of the Holy Spirit in their lives. Acts helps us better understand how the things mentioned in the Old Testament came true through New Testament events. This book is proof that Jesus lived, died on the cross, and rose again, and that people believed in him so much, they were willing to risk their lives. If Jesus were a myth or fairy tale, there would be no book of Acts.

## Early Days of the Church

Acts has three parts that tell us how the church started and grew. The first part includes the resurrected Jesus meeting with his family, the disciples (now called apostles), and other followers. This part also shows that after Jesus returned to heaven, the Holy Spirit came to give power to Peter and the believers. In the second part of Acts, Saul persecutes the Christians, then becomes a Christian himself and calls himself Paul. The third part is about Paul's missionary journeys to establish the church.

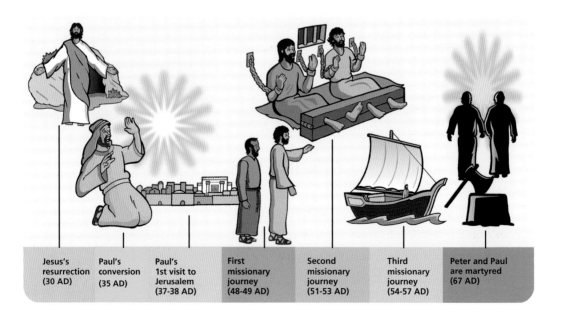

| Jesus's resurrection (30 AD) | Paul's conversion (35 AD) | Paul's 1st visit to Jerusalem (37-38 AD) | First missionary journey (48-49 AD) | Second missionary journey (51-53 AD) | Third missionary journey (54-57 AD) | Peter and Paul are martyred (67 AD) |

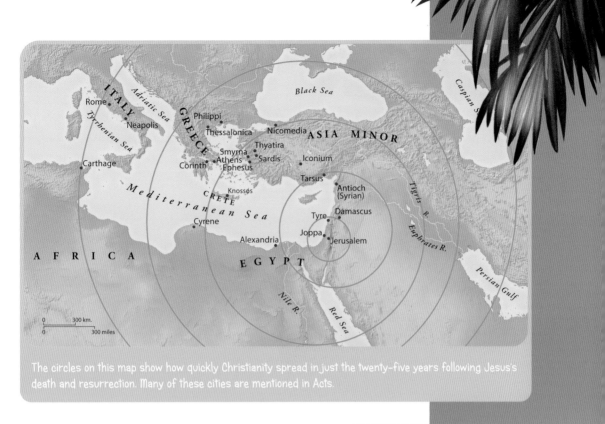

The circles on this map show how quickly Christianity spread in just the twenty-five years following Jesus's death and resurrection. Many of these cities are mentioned in Acts.

## Faith Founded on Fact

As a doctor and believer, Luke traveled with Paul and served as a physician to the group that went with them. Luke was an eyewitness to many events in the early church. He also knew eyewitnesses to the life, death, and resurrection of Jesus, which he wrote about in Luke. We can trust the events Luke wrote about in Acts really happened because so many facts are included.

## Acts and the New Testament

Part of Acts includes Paul's missionary journeys. On these trips, Paul started churches in cities throughout the Roman Empire. Later, Paul wrote letters to these churches, which are also part of the New Testament.

As you read through Acts, look for times when God changed ordinary people into powerful messengers of the gospel who were:

1. Preaching sermons to crowds

2. Sharing the gospel with religious leaders

3. Taking the gospel to unbelievers

4. Meeting the needs of the church

5. Serving fellow believers

6. Speaking truth to government authorities

# Romans

The Roman Empire ruled the world. All eyes were on the city of Rome, where the emperor lived and reigned. It was here in the heart of the most powerful political spot on the planet that God established a church. How did this church get started? Were there Jews from Rome who visited Jerusalem at Pentecost, heard Peter's sermon, and were among the three thousand people who got saved that day? Did a disciple travel to Rome and start a church? Did Christians move to Rome and take their faith with them? We don't know for sure. What we do know is that a church started in Rome soon after Jesus's resurrection. Paul hoped to visit it one day. He wrote a letter to the church of Rome that eventually became this book we now call Romans.

## A Magnum Opus

What is a magnum opus? It is someone's most important achievement or work. The book of Romans has been called Paul's magnum opus. It's the most important letter he wrote to the churches because it has valuable information about doctrines, which are core beliefs of Christianity. Romans is a fantastic book to read if you want to grow stronger in your faith!

iStock.com/CosmoPic

This paved road leading into Rome is the Appian Way. You can still walk on it today, just like Paul did!

Many Christians in Rome secretly gathered in the catacombs—underground tunnels and caves where the dead were buried. Some Roman emperors arrested and persecuted Christians, so it was a safer place to meet.

iStock.com/frankix

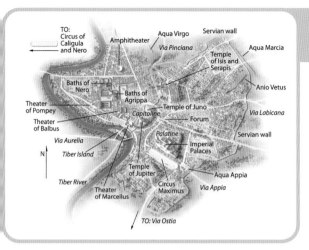

TO:
Circus of
Caligula
and Nero

Amphitheater
Aqua Virgo
Servian wall
Via Pinciana
Temple
of Isis and
Serapis
Aqua Marcia

Baths of
Nero
Baths of
Agrippa
Anio Vetus

Theater
of Pompey
Capitoline
Temple of Juno
Via Labicana

Theater
of Balbus
Forum

Via Aurelia
Palatine
Servian wall

Tiber Island
Imperial
Palaces

N
Temple
of Jupiter
Aqua Appia

Tiber River
Circus
Maximus
Via Appia

Theater
of Marcellus

TO: Via Ostia

## Big Words to Know

Romans covers a lot of important topics that sound like really big words. Check out the graphic to see what some of these big words mean, especially to Christians.

**Righteousness:** God's holy and right actions, perfect and without sin.

**Justification:** When God says someone is right and good because they choose to believe in the death and resurrection of Jesus and follow him as Lord of their life. It's "just-as-if" they'd never sinned!

**Sanctification:** Growing to be more and more like Jesus after someone becomes a Christian.

Do you have questions? The book of Romans has answers! Here are some to look for as you read through this book.

**Q: What does it mean to be a Christian?**
A: Read Romans 1:16-17

**Q: What does God say about people who have never heard about Jesus?**
A: Read Romans 1:18-20

**Q: What if bad things happen to us? Does it mean God doesn't care?**
A: Read Romans 8:28

**Q: Can a Christian be separated from God's love?**
A: Read Romans 8:37-38

95

# 1 Corinthians

The apostle Paul was like a gardener—he planted things. But instead of fruits and vegetables, he planted churches. Just like any gardener, Paul took care of what he planted—he helped the new churches follow God better. Paul planted a church in the city of Corinth, then wrote letters to help them with their issues. He also encouraged them to grow in faith and be more like Jesus in everything they did. Those letters are in the Bible as 1 and 2 Corinthians. They still help us today!

Corinth was in Greece, the country that held the ancient Olympics. In 1 Corinthians 9:24–25, Paul encouraged the Corinthian church to pursue God and his holy ways with the same determination as an athlete competing for first place.

## Problems

Paul visited the Greek city of Corinth on his second missionary journey. He found a town full of people who followed sinful pagan practices. When Paul preached the gospel to them, many repented of their sins and chose to follow Jesus as their Lord and Savior. Along with these new Christians, Paul established the church in Corinth. But after he left to continue his journey, Paul heard reports of problems in the church and wrote this letter to help the Corinthians. The first part of 1 Corinthians explains what to do when there are arguments and divisions in the church. The second part of this book explains what to do when Christians continue to sin and aren't living holy lives. The third part of this book answers different questions the church had.

The carvings of these menorahs—the Hebrew word for *candelabra* or *lampstand*—are from an ancient synagogue (a Jewish place of worship) in Corinth. As he usually did, Paul preached first in Corinth's synagogue before taking his message to the Gentiles.

William D. Mounce

## Teaching Truth

Paul grew up as a Jew who was taught to live a godly life by following the Ten Commandments and the Jewish scriptures. The Corinthians worshiped Greek gods and learned Greek philosophy. Many didn't understand the basic differences between right and wrong. In this book, Paul teaches the truth about living God's way. Staying pure, honoring marriage, and living a moral life were some of the truths Paul taught. Praying in public, using spiritual gifts, and how to hold church services were also a priority on his list.

Paul wrote this letter to the Corinth church while he was living in Ephesus.

## The Love List

First Corinthians 13 is one of the most important (and famous!) chapters in the Bible. It has a list of what real love looks like and acts like. This list helps us learn how to show love to others. It also shows us what God's love is like. Most of all, it teaches us that love is the greatest thing of all.

LOVE IS

patient
not self-seeking
kind
not easily angered
not envious
forgiving
humble
God-honoring
modest
truthful
trusting
protecting of others

# 2 Corinthians

Paul wrote another letter to the church in Corinth that is now known as 2 Corinthians. This church continued to have problems, but Paul continued to help them. He showed them what Jesus actually taught and who he was, and how to follow God's holy ways of living.

## Forgiveness

Paul experienced Jesus's forgiveness when he became a Christian. In 1 Corinthians, he told people to repent of their sins so they could be forgiven. Now in 2 Corinthians, Paul asked the church to forgive others as well.

## The Judgment Seat

There was a platform in Corinth called the judgment seat. It was like a courtroom. Angry Jews brought Paul here and accused him of breaking the law by preaching about Jesus. Paul wrote that one day we will all stand before Christ's judgment seat. Jesus will examine the good and bad things we have done.

© 1995 Phoenix Data Systems

This stone platform in Corinth was called the judgment seat.

## The Apostle Paul

Paul's authority as an apostle—a leader in the church—was being questioned. In 2 Corinthians, Paul explains why he was qualified. He details how he was put in prison, beaten, and stoned. He was shipwrecked three times! He spent an entire night and day floating in the ocean before he was rescued. He experienced hunger, thirst, cold, and sleepless nights. Once, he escaped by hiding inside a basket and being lowered out a window to the ground below. Through it all, Paul said God encouraged him and strengthened him to continue in his ministry.

## Key City

Corinth was one of the most important cities of its day because it was a great location for trade and travel. Due to its long and interesting history, Julius Caesar had rebuilt it and established it as the capital of its province in the Roman Empire. Corinth was a symbol of riches, luxurious living, and wrongdoing. Paul and the early church leaders worked hard to help the new believers in Corinth live new lives for Christ.

## Helping People in Need

How does God want us to give to people who need help? As you read through 2 Corinthians, look for some of these guidelines on giving.

1. Even if you don't have much money, you can still give to someone in need (2 Corinthians 8:1–3).
2. Jesus was an example we should follow (2 Corinthians 8:7–9).
3. People with a generous, giving heart will experience many blessings (2 Corinthians 9:6).
4. God loves those who give with a cheerful heart (2 Corinthians 9:8).
5. We can share with others because God provides everything we need (2 Corinthians 9:10).

Paul established the Corinthian church on his second missionary journey.

# Galatians

The churches in Galatia had a problem. Some of their leaders said people had to follow all of God's laws if they wanted to be saved and go to heaven when they died. Why was this a problem? Because that would mean our salvation depends on our own actions. As Paul pointed out in this book, that's not the true gospel message. The gospel tells us Jesus did all the work for us. He died on the cross to pay the penalty for our sins, then he offered us salvation as a gift. It's free! Only faith in Jesus can save us. That's what the book of Galatians is all about.

## The Ten Commandments

If the Ten Commandments can't save us, do we even need to read them? Yes! Paul explains in Galatians that the Ten Commandments do a very special job. God's law is our teacher. It teaches us right from wrong. It teaches us we need Jesus to save us from the wrong things we do. The Ten Commandments help point us to Jesus!

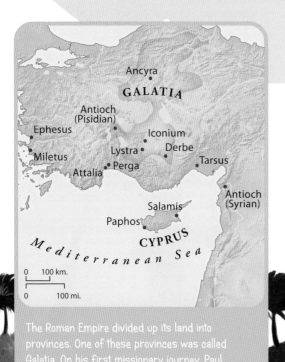

The Roman Empire divided up its land into provinces. One of these provinces was called Galatia. On his first missionary journey, Paul planted churches in Galatia.

The region known as Galatia during Paul's day is in the area we now call Turkey.

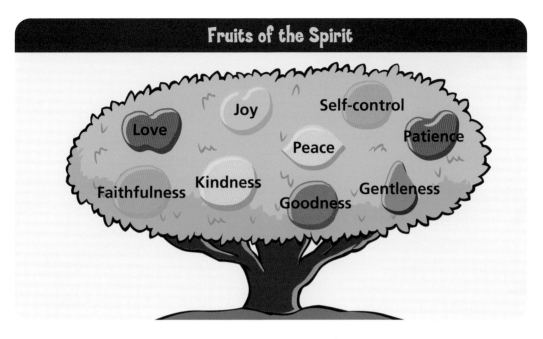

## Fruits of the Spirit

Self-control
Joy
Love
Peace
Patience
Kindness
Faithfulness
Gentleness
Goodness

## Growing with God

Galatians contains a lot of opposites. Paul wanted to compare and contrast different things to show the churches in Galatia how to grow in their faith. For example, there are right or wrong choices we can make in the way we live and act toward others. When we make the right choices, it shows the Spirit of God is growing good fruit—or qualities—in our lives. Ask God to grow these fruits in your heart.

## Facts About Galatia

The Celts were people from ancient Europe. They left their original homes and villages and settled in many different areas. Some moved toward the west and settled in parts of Great Britain and Ireland. Others settled in France and parts of Belgium, Germany, and Italy. The Celts from those last areas were known as Gauls. The Gauls also moved into what is modern-day Turkey. They conquered the people living there and named the area after themselves. When the Roman Empire marched in and took control, they named this region Galatia, along with the nearby cities. Paul visited the cities in Galatia on his first missionary journey and planted churches in that Roman province.

# Ephesians

Ephesians can be divided into two parts. In the first half, Paul explains important doctrines (guiding beliefs) every Christian should know. In the second half, Paul describes what the life of a Christian looks like. The first three chapters of Ephesians help everyone in the church stand on a firm foundation of truth. The second three chapters help everyone in the church grow to be more like Jesus.

## The Church in Ephesus

We can discover more about the church in Ephesus by reading other parts of the Bible. In Acts 19, we learn that Paul traveled by road to arrive at Ephesus, an important seaport city in a Roman province called Asia (which is different from what we call Asia today). At first Paul taught in the local synagogue, but when most of the members rejected his words, he moved to a different place to teach the good news to the Gentiles. The church in Ephesus was then born. Eventually, through Paul's preaching, all the Jews and Greeks in the Asia province heard the gospel.

> Roman soldiers marched throughout the empire of Rome. Paul knew his readers would be very familiar with the armor they wore, which may be why he used it to explain the spiritual things Christians should "put on" each day.

## Walk in Love

Paul wanted Christians to walk in love. What does this look like? As you read through Ephesians, look for ways Paul encouraged the church to act toward others so that you, too, can walk in love.

- Speak the truth (Ephesians 4:25).
- Honor your parents (Ephesians 6:2).
- Sing praises and thanksgiving to God (Ephesians 5:19–20).
- Learn to control your anger (Ephesians 4:26–27).
- Be kind, compassionate, and forgiving (Ephesians 4:32).
- Live a moral, pure, and holy life (Ephesians 5:3–7).

## Magic and Sorcery

A number of people in Ephesus were involved with dark magic and sorcery. After they heard about Jesus, they repented of the wrong things they'd done and became Christians. They brought their books and scrolls of magic and sorcery to a public place and burned them because they no longer wanted to read them or practice the evil things they taught.

## Armor of God

When Paul wrote Ephesians, he was a prisoner in Rome. During his imprisonment, he was guarded by a Roman soldier. Paul probably examined the soldier's armor closely. He used this example to encourage Christians to put on the whole armor of God and stand strong in their faith.

Ephesus was a key port city used by both the Greeks and Romans. Its harbor eventually filled up with silt (mud), making it not as important anymore.

© 2012 by Zondervan

The ruins of this ancient Ephesian theater were the scene of a riot against Paul because he was preaching that people should worship Jesus instead of idols. Local silverworkers who made idols lost a lot of income when people in Ephesus began following Jesus.

# Philippians

Rejoice in the Lord always! That was Paul's message in this letter to the church in Philippi. Paul had experience with the difficulties and sufferings that can come from following Christ. Because they cast a demon out of a slave girl, Paul and Silas were beaten and thrown into prison in Philippi. Yet that very same evening, Paul and Silas sang hymns to God. Yes, they were still in jail. Yes, they were still bound in chains. But they still chose to worship God in their hour of need. The result? The jailer and his entire household became believers! And they were filled with joy!

## Who Is Jesus?

In Philippians, Paul gives different descriptions of who Jesus is.

### Jesus Is . . .

- our life (see 1:21)
- our comfort (see 2:1)
- the perfect model of humility (see 2:8)
- our righteousness (see 3:9)
- our peace (see 4:7)
- the power and strength we need in any situation (see 4:13)

## Let's Learn More!

To learn more about Paul's first visit to Philippi and the people he met there, read Acts 16:11–40. You'll meet Lydia, a businesswoman. Plus, you'll get to know the jailer of the local prison. Most important of all, you'll learn what happened to them and how they made the decision to believe in Jesus.

> The first person to respond to the gospel in Philippi was Lydia, who bought and sold purple cloth. In New Testament times, only the very wealthy could afford clothes dyed purple.

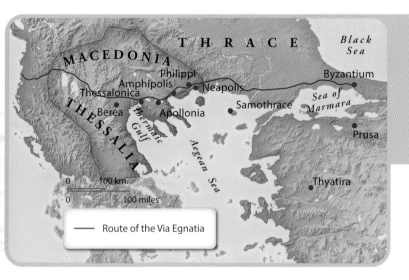

The main road, called the Egnatian Way (or Via Egnatia), connected the Adriatic Sea with the city of Byzantium. It passed through such cities as Philippi and Thessalonica. Paul probably walked along this ancient Roman road.

## The Church at Philippi

Philippi was a Roman colony with a military outpost. However, there was no synagogue in the city for Paul to visit. Instead, he went with Silas to a place by the river where people met to pray. That's where he met Lydia. She believed the gospel message she heard from Paul and became the first member of the new church he planted there. Others soon believed too, and the church was formed.

### Encouragement

As you read through Philippians, look for ways God wants to strengthen and encourage you. Memorize the verses that help you the most.

- When you feel discouraged, read Philippians 1:6.
- When you feel confused, read Philippians 1:9–11.
- When you feel afraid to share your faith, read Philippians 1:14.
- When you feel afraid of death, read Philippians 1:21.
- When you feel proud, read Philippians 2:3–4.
- When you feel anxious or depressed, read Philippians 4:4–7.
- When you feel overwhelmed with bad thoughts, read Philippians 4:8.
- When you feel discontented, read Philippians 4:11–13.

# Colossians

Just like the book of Ephesians, Colossians can be divided into two parts. The first half explains important doctrines (major beliefs) of Christian faith. The second half gives examples of how to live out this faith. What key doctrine does Paul focus on in the first part of this book? Paul teaches that Jesus is God. How does this knowledge make a difference in our lives? People who follow Christ will stop doing the sinful things they used to do. Instead, they will walk in Jesus's footsteps. They will live a holy life everywhere they go and in everything they do.

## Jesus Is God

It is important to be part of a church that teaches the main truths found in the Bible. Some people say Jesus is only a special teacher. Others say he is a god, but not as powerful or as important as God. In Colossians, Paul explains that Jesus *is* God. As part of the Trinity, Jesus is the creator of the universe. He is the power that holds the universe together. He is the one who brings peace between God and people. We don't have to just take Paul's word for it, though. Throughout the Bible, there is solid evidence that Jesus is God.

- Jesus himself said he is God (John 10:30).
- Doubters changed their mind to believe Jesus is God (John 20:24–29).
- Enemies tried to kill Jesus for claiming to be God (John 10:33).
- Jesus's own brothers believed Jesus is God (James 1:1 and Jude 4).
- Eyewitness to his ministry and life declared Jesus is God (2 Peter 1:1).

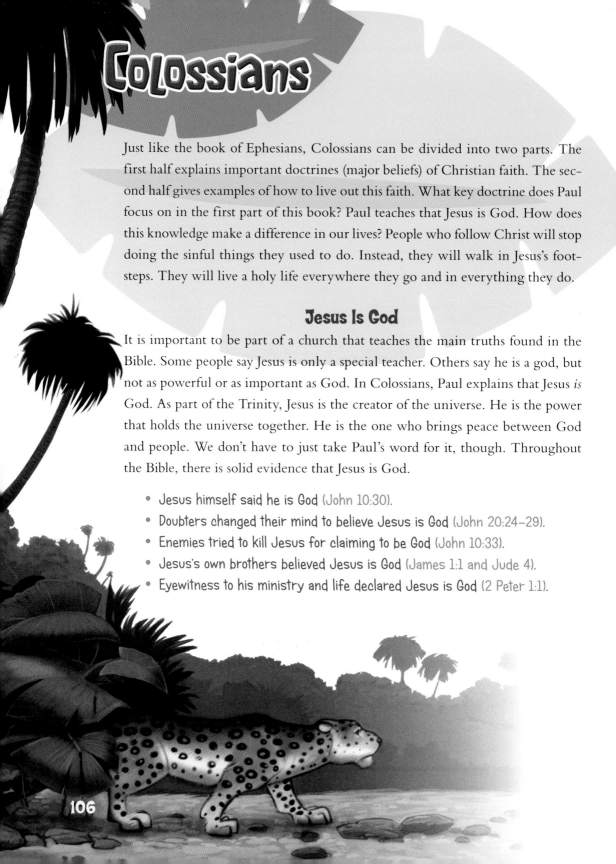

Clinton E. Arnold

## More than a Mailman

Tychicus was Paul's mailman. He carried Paul's letters to the churches in Ephesus and Colossae. But Tychicus was more than just a letter carrier. He was Paul's close friend and a fellow worker for Christ. When he arrived at a church with Paul's letter, he didn't simply read it aloud to people. Tychicus also encouraged them. He stepped in to lead them so their leaders could join Paul in his ministry to other churches. In Colossians 4:7, Paul calls Tychicus a close brother, faithful minister, and fellow servant in the Lord.

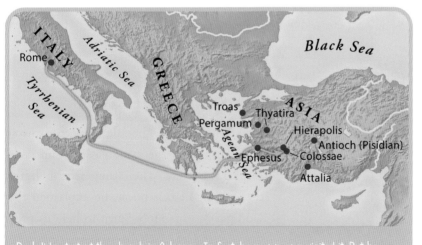

# 1 Thessalonians

As was his custom, Paul first preached at the synagogue in Thessalonica. So many people believed in the gospel message that the synagogue's leaders grew angry and organized violent mobs against Paul and his friends. The book of 1 Thessalonians was written to a church that was experiencing persecution. Paul reminded them that suffering and persecution will come to those who follow Jesus. He also urged them to find joy in the knowledge Jesus will come again.

## Follow the Leader!

Paul opened 1 Thessalonians with a greeting from himself, Silas, and Timothy. He was grateful the believers in Thessalonica were following their lead and imitating their actions. As you read through 1 Thessalonians, and especially chapter 2, look for ways that you can follow the example of these godly Christians as well.

- Share the gospel with boldness.
- Try to please God instead of others.
- Be gentle and kind toward other people.
- Work hard when you have responsibilities.
- Act in ways that are holy, blameless, and good.

## Self-Control

Paul inspired the Thessalonians to grow in their faith with the same passion and dedication they had when they first believed the gospel. In this book, he explained that God gave us his Holy Spirit to help us grow stronger and learn self-control over our bodies

Parts of Thessalonica have been excavated, and the remains of original buildings can be seen today.

eFesenko/Shutterstock.com

108

and our thoughts. Paul reminded the church to live like people who know God and want to honor him.

## Changed Forever!

In 1 Thessalonians, Paul assured the believers that he is confident in their strong faith. He saw them stop worshiping idols and instead worship the true God. He knew they believed the gospel is the Word of God, and that they were filled with power from the Holy Spirit. They were also eagerly waiting for Jesus to return. Their lives would never be the same after hearing and believing the good news about Jesus.

## He's Coming Back!

Jesus told the disciples he would come back again. When he does, we will be with him forever. In this book, Paul provides many details about important events that will take place when Jesus returns. Paul also encouraged the believers to comfort each other by talking about how wonderful it will be. Read 1 Thessalonians 5:1–11 to learn more.

# 2 Thessalonians

Paul was like a father to the churches he established. He felt love and concern for each new believer, even when he was away from them. When he heard the church in Thessalonica was having a problem, Paul wrote them this letter that is now called 2 Thessalonians. What was the problem? They'd been listening to wrong ideas about the coming day of the Lord.

## The Day of the Lord

God is a just and fair God. The Bible teaches that one day he will judge the world. He will punish those who delight in wickedness and he will reward those who delight in good. This day of judgment is known as the "day of the Lord." The church in Thessalonica thought the day of judgment had already started. But Paul set them straight. He explained in this book that it would not start until certain events took place.

## An Example to Follow

Another report reached Paul about the believers in Thessalonica. Some people refused to work. They ate food without paying for it. They made things harder for other people. In short, they were busybodies. Paul urged the church to act differently. Paul and his missionary team worked hard to earn money to buy their own food so they would not be a burden on anyone. They made themselves an example for everyone to follow.

Thessalonica was a valuable port city with a busy harbor during the days of the early church.

110

# Encouragement

The book of 2 Thessalonians has words of encouragement for the church today, especially as we draw closer to the Lord's coming. As you read, look for ways God wants to encourage everyone who believes in him.

- God gives us rest and relief from our troubles (2 Thessalonians 1:7).
- God's power will help us do good things in our lives (2 Thessalonians 1:11).
- The Holy Spirit is working inside us for good (2 Thessalonians 2:13).
- Jesus gives us hope (2 Thessalonians 2:16).
- Jesus will strengthen us to do good in both our thoughts and our actions. (2 Thessalonians 2:17).
- Jesus gives us peace (2 Thessalonians 3:16).

Thessalonica was a city in the Macedonian province of the Roman Empire. This map shows where it was located alongside other cities Paul wrote to.

# 1 Timothy

Many books in the New Testament first started as letters to the churches, but 1 Timothy was a letter to a specific person. Timothy was a man Paul trained to be a pastor and leader in the church in Ephesus. Paul wrote to Timothy to teach him how to handle different problems the church was having.

## Meet Timothy

Timothy was still young when he stepped into a leadership position, but he had grown up in a family that believed in God. His mother, Eunice, and his grandmother, Lois, taught him the Old Testament Scriptures when he was a boy. When Timothy heard the gospel message, he decided to follow Christ. Paul was so impressed by Timothy's strong faith and godly example that he invited Timothy to join his second missionary journey. From then on, Paul trained Timothy to be a leader in the church. Timothy is even mentioned as a coauthor in some of Paul's letters. Paul was close to Timothy and talked to him like he was a son.

This mosaic is of the widow Jesus praised when she gave an offering even though she had little money. Paul instructed Timothy on how the church should take care of widows who had no family to provide for them.

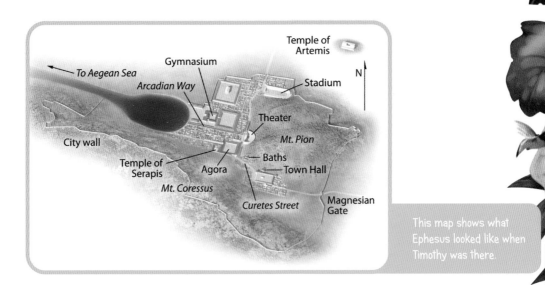

Temple of
Artemis

To Aegean Sea

Gymnasium

Arcadian Way

Stadium

N

Theater

City wall

Mt. Pion

Temple of
Serapis

Baths

Agora

Town Hall

Mt. Coressus

Curetes Street

Magnesian
Gate

This map shows what
Ephesus looked like when
Timothy was there.

## Used by God

Timothy was young, but Paul was confident he could do the job. How? By using the spiritual gifts God had given him, by praying, and by living a godly life. Even though you are young, God can use you too! Look for ways God encourages you and strengthens you to do important things in your daily life.

## A Final Warning

Paul ends his letter by warning Timothy not to get caught up in arguments or pointless discussions, and not to be fooled by false teachings. Paul urged Timothy to focus on knowing God instead. Read 1 Timothy 6:20–21 to learn more.

## Building the Church

As a leader in the Ephesian church, Timothy dealt with many different issues. Paul wrote this letter to give him advice on:

- The importance of prayer
- The example of godly women
- Choosing leaders in the church
- Dealing with false teachings
- Using spiritual gifts
- Treating widows and the older members well
- Working with the poor and the rich in the church

# 2 Timothy

Second Timothy was the last letter Paul wrote. He penned it from inside a Roman prison, and he was probably put to death soon after he finished. Even though Paul was suffering in prison, he wrote this letter to encourage Timothy! Paul knew his ministry was ending, but he was filled with hope that Timothy would continue to spread the good news about Jesus. Aware of the hardships Timothy was experiencing as a church leader, Paul wanted to reassure Timothy and cheer him up. Paul's words encouraged and strengthened Timothy, and they can encourage and strengthen us today.

## Always Be Ready

In 2 Timothy 4:2, Paul tells Timothy to be ready to preach the word "in season and out of season." What does this mean? It could be Paul saying Timothy would benefit from reading the Bible regularly. If we do the same thing, we will be prepared like Timothy was with the tools we need when God brings us unexpected opportunities to share the gospel with others.

## Exciting Examples

In 2 Timothy, Paul used many exciting examples to compare to the life of a Christian.

**A soldier training for battle**
2 Timothy 2:3–4

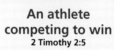

**An athlete competing to win**
2 Timothy 2:5

**A farmer patiently waiting to harvest the crops**
2 Timothy 2:6

**A hardworking and honest worker**
2 Timothy 2:15

**A valuable vessel of gold or silver**
2 Timothy 2:20–21

**A trusted servant of the Lord**
2 Timothy 2:24–26

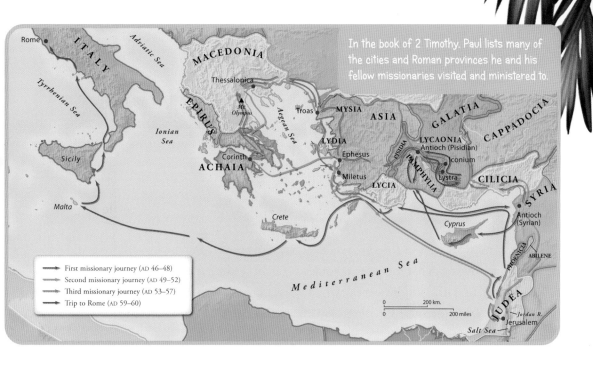

In the book of 2 Timothy, Paul lists many of the cities and Roman provinces he and his fellow missionaries visited and ministered to.

First missionary journey (AD 46–48)
Second missionary journey (AD 49–52)
Third missionary journey (AD 53–57)
Trip to Rome (AD 59–60)

## Strength in the Lord

Paul knew what it was like to suffer as a Christian. He also knew how to find strength when he felt weak. In 2 Timothy 4:17, Paul shares that God stood beside him in times of need, by giving him the strength to preach the gospel message to others and delivering him from danger and dangerous people. Paul encouraged Timothy to also find his strength in God.

In this letter, Paul described the sad details of his imprisonment. He was in chains. He was alone, with only Luke to help him. He wanted Timothy to bring him his cloak, books, and parchments.

Paul's message is important to us too. Do you feel weak in your faith? Do you feel like you don't know how to tell others about Jesus? Ask God to be with you and strengthen you, just as he did Paul.

## Pastoral Letters

Three of Paul's letters have instructions for leaders of the early church. These are 1 Timothy, 2 Timothy, and Titus. These books have instructions on how to oversee a church, encouragement for church leaders, and advice on dealing with problems in the church.

# Titus

Paul wrote this book as a letter to Titus, his helper and fellow missionary. Earlier, Paul and Titus had visited the island of Crete. When Paul continued on his journeys, however, he left Titus in charge of the churches there. Paul used this letter to encourage Titus as a church leader, warn him about people who taught false things about following Jesus, and teach him how to raise up godly leaders and members in the church.

## Good Works

Will our good works get us into heaven? No. Titus 3:4–7 says the good work Jesus did on the cross will save us. That means everyone who believes in Jesus as their Lord and Savior will be saved. In Titus 3:8, however, we learn that believers should also be careful to do good works. Why? Because showing God's love through our actions is good for others, and it's good for us.

## The Holy Spirit

God does not expect us to do good works all on our own. In Titus 3:5–6, he promises to pour the Holy Spirit out on us . . . in abundance! Pray and ask God to wash and renew you with the power of the Holy Spirit today.

This building in Crete, called the Basilica of Titus, is dedicated to Titus and the good works he did on the island.

Andrei Nekrassov/Shutterstock.com

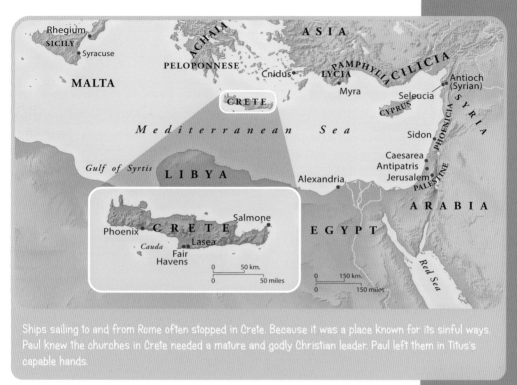

Ships sailing to and from Rome often stopped in Crete. Because it was a place known for its sinful ways, Paul knew the churches in Crete needed a mature and godly Christian leader. Paul left them in Titus's capable hands.

## Godly Living

Paul gives Titus specific instructions for choosing leaders to serve in the church. Paul also lists examples of good works and godly living that are good for every Christian to follow. What good works would you like to do? Pray and ask God to help you grow!

- Be welcoming to others.
- Love the good things God loves.
- Be just, fair, and honest.
- Exercise self-control.
- Always follow the Bible's teaching and sound doctrine.
- Honor your family and authority figures.
- Be a good example for others to follow.
- Be enthusiastic and passionate about doing good works for God.

# Philemon

The books of Philemon and Colossians were probably written around the same time. But while Colossians was written to the church in the city of Colossae, Philemon was a letter written mainly to one person—a man in Colossae named Philemon. Who was Philemon? We don't know much about him, but Paul mentions there was a church that met in his house. Paul also addressed his letter to this church.

## Meet Onesimus

What is the story behind this book? There was a man named Onesimus who worked as a slave in Philemon's home. Unhappy with his situation, Onesimus ran away and may even have stolen money. While Onesimus was traveling from Colossae to Rome, he heard Paul preach the gospel message and became a Christian! Onesimus then decided to return to Philemon and face the consequences of his actions. Paul wrote this letter to appeal to Philemon on Onesimus's behalf.

A church in the city of Colossae met in the home of Philemon.

## Slavery

God values every person's life. In Galatians 3:28, Paul explains that everyone is equal in Christ's eyes. Sadly, all throughout history and even today, some people have forced other people to live without freedoms or basic rights. Different cultures have given different degrees of freedom to the people they enslaved, but any form of slavery goes against the true message of the gospel. In verses 15–16, Paul asks Philemon to take Onesimus back— not as a slave, but as a brother in Christ.

## Forgiveness

Philemon is a very short letter, but it carries a very big message. It's all about forgiveness. Paul asks Philemon to forgive Onesimus for anything he may have done wrong or anything of value he may have taken. This message was written to one person, but it speaks to all of us today. Is there someone you need to forgive? Talk with a trusted adult about it. Read verses in the Bible about it. Pray about it. Ask God to help you be loving and forgiving and wise.

### Forgiveness in Christ

This book teaches us how to forgive another person, but it also teaches us about how Jesus forgives us:

- We are guilty of sinning against God (verse 11).
- Jesus prays for us (verses 9–10).
- Jesus put aside his heavenly glory to come as our Savior (verses 8–9).
- On the cross, Jesus paid the debt for our sins (verse 18).
- Because of Jesus, we are restored to a right relationship with God (verses 15–16).

# Hebrews

The book of Hebrews is a treasure chest waiting for you to open it! It's rich with nuggets of spiritual gold such as God's promises, exciting examples of faith, and hope for every believer. So get ready for adventure. Get ready to explore. Get ready to draw closer to Jesus and grow stronger in your faith!

## Jesus, the Best of All!

Who wrote Hebrews? Since there is no name signed to this book, nobody knows for sure. But we do know who Hebrews was written for. This book was a letter to the Hebrews—or Jews—who had become followers of Jesus. As you read Hebrews, look for how it compares Jesus to many people the Jews were already familiar with: priests, Moses, and even angels. Hebrews says Jesus is better than any of these. Why? Because Jesus is the best of all!

## Warning! Danger Ahead!

Hebrews also has important warnings about the dangers believers should stay away from. It teaches us what to do to stay strong in our faith. Look for these warnings as you read:

- Pay attention to the Bible and the message of salvation. (See Hebrews 2:1–4.)
- Follow God willingly, not with a stubborn heart. (See Hebrews 3:7–4:13.)
- Do all you can to grow stronger in your faith every day. (See Hebrews 5:11–6:20.)
- When you sin, ask God to forgive you and help you be more like Jesus. (See Hebrews 10:26–39.)
- Accept the truth of God's word in the Bible. (See Hebrews 12:25–29.)

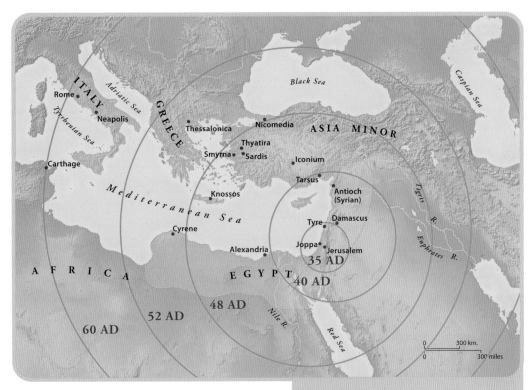

## Faith Hall of Fame

Hebrews has a chapter that's often called the Faith Hall of Fame. Starting with Abel, the son of Adam and Eve, it lists men and women throughout the history of the Bible who are remembered as heroes because of their faith. The exciting thing is we can be heroes too! How? By following their examples. Most of all, we can look to Jesus as the author and finisher of our faith—the one who truly shows us how it's done. Read Hebrews 11:1–12:2 to learn more.

Jewish Christians lived throughout the Roman Empire, not just in Jerusalem. This map shows where Christianity was practiced over time.

121

# James

What Proverbs is to the Old Testament, James is to the New Testament. This book gave practical advice to the early church, particularly Jews who had become Christians, and it also offers helpful advice to Christians today. The author of this book is James, who was one of Jesus's brothers. As an important leader in the early church in Jerusalem, he had many valuable lessons to teach the young believers.

## Jesus's Family

When you study the Gospels, the first four books of the New Testament, you'll discover facts about Jesus's family! Joseph and Mary had four sons and at least two daughters. Jesus's younger half brothers were James, Joseph, Simon, and Judas (also called Jude). We don't know the names of his half sisters. Read Mark 6:3 and Matthew 13:55–56 to learn more.

## Trials

When someone becomes a Christian, it doesn't mean their lives will be perfect from that point on. What it does mean is when trials and difficult times come in a Christian's life, God is there to help. In this book, James encourages us when we find ourselves in the middle of a trial. He says that when we go through a trial, we will grow in our faith. Trials are like spiritual exercises that teach us and help us grow strong.

## Did You Know?

A Jewish historian named Josephus wrote about James in his history book. Sources like this from outside the Bible show our faith is founded on actual facts in history.

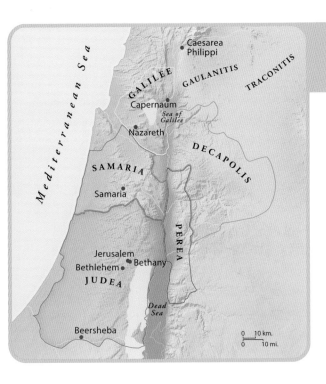

This map shows Israel during the life of James in the first century, when it was under control of the Roman Empire.

## Temptation

Every Christian deals with temptation. The book of James offers practical advice on how to handle temptation in your life. One of the most important things to know about temptation, however, is that God will never tempt us. Read James 1:13–17 to learn more.

## The Tongue

One of the most famous passages in James is about the tongue. James 3:1–12 teaches us that our words are important—they can bless people or hurt them. Even though the tongue is a small part of our body, it can cause a lot of healing or a lot of pain. Our words show what's in our heart. James challenges us to have a good heart and speak words that are kind and true.

## Powerful Prayers

James 5:16 teaches us that the prayers of righteous people (those who do what is right) are powerful and effective. Do you feel like you are a righteous person? Romans 5:1 says that every believer has been made right with God through what Jesus did for us on the cross. Whether you feel righteous or not, if you are a Christian, you are righteous in God's eyes. This means that when you pray, your prayers are packed with a powerful punch against the kingdom of darkness and evil!

# 1 Peter

The early churches were under persecution. Christians were being punished because they worshiped Jesus. The Roman Empire demanded that people worship Caesar instead. Jesus's disciple Simon Peter wrote this book to encourage the believers who were suffering. He explained how to find hope and live holy lives even when times get tough.

## Finding Hope

Where can we find this hope when things get hard? Peter says it comes through salvation in Jesus. Just like the early Christians, we can call to Jesus, ask forgiveness for our sins, and invite him to be our Lord and Savior. Give Jesus all your questions and worries and ask him to send his Holy Spirit to comfort you, encourage you, and make you strong. You can also read your Bible to learn more about his promises and plans for your life.

## Do Unto Others

God cares about how we care for others. First Peter gives many examples of how God wants us to treat other people.

- Love others and be kind. (See 1 Peter 1:22.)
- Be glad for what others have, and be content with what is yours. (See 1 Peter 2:1.)
- Honor others because everyone is important to God. (See 1 Peter 2:17.)
- Help others who are in need. (See 1 Peter 3:8.)
- Be courteous and polite to others, not rude. (See 1 Peter 3:9.)
- Spend time with others who make godly choices and don't hang out with people who do wrong things. (See 1 Peter 4:1–5.)
- Welcome others with friendly words. (See 1 Peter 4:9.)

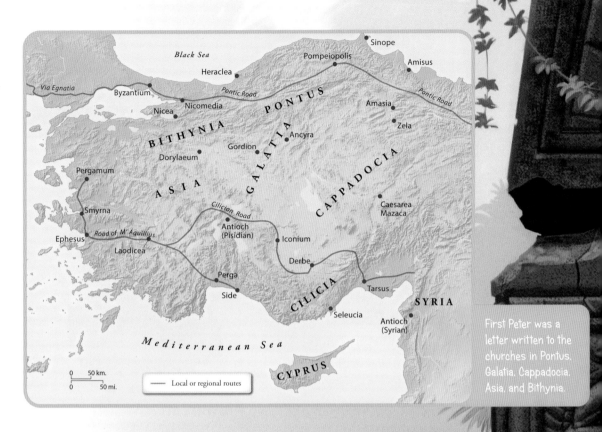

First Peter was a letter written to the churches in Pontus, Galatia, Cappadocia, Asia, and Bithynia.

## Obey God

When Peter and the other apostles told people about Jesus, they were put in jail and ordered to stop preaching. But they knew they had to obey God's laws instead of people's rules, so they never stopped teaching about Jesus.

In this book, Peter talks about the importance of obeying authority—like governments and leaders. But when those in authority say things that go against the Bible, we can remember what Peter and the apostles did. It's important to obey God's laws as the most important laws of all. Read Acts 5:17–42 and 1 Peter 2:17–25 to learn more.

# 2 Peter

This book was a letter that was sent to Christians everywhere. Peter warned believers not to listen to false teachers. These people were teaching doctrines Jesus never taught. Peter explained that Jesus's real disciples weren't following clever fables or made-up stories. They were eyewitnesses. They had seen Jesus in person and witnessed his majesty and miracles.

## Filled with Power

Peter had been a fisherman on the Sea of Galilee . . . until he met Jesus. Then he and his brother Andrew became disciples. After Jesus's death and resurrection, Peter became the leader of the twelve apostles (original disciples). Through knowing Jesus and with the power of the Holy Spirit, Peter went from a person without much education to a powerful preacher of the gospel. Do you feel like an ordinary kid? Ask Jesus to fill you with the Holy Spirit and use you in powerful ways . . . just like Peter!

## Growing in Your Faith

Pray for the Holy Spirit to grow the fruit of the Spirit in your heart so you can love others like Jesus does.

Be kind to others and look for ways you can share God's love.

Read the Bible to learn how to make godly choices and live a holy life.

Learn as much as you can about Jesus and what it means to be a Christian.

Make the decision to have faith in Jesus as your Lord and Savior.

## Let's Grow!

A tiny acorn becomes a big oak tree slowly over many years after it's planted, living in good and bad weather as it grows from small shoots into a tall tree with branches and leaves. Then it makes acorns of its own.

How does a Christian grow? A lot like a tree! Peter tells us how to grow, step by step. Read 2 Peter 1:5–9 to learn more.

This map shows the area of Galilee, where Peter lived and did his ministry.

This copy of 2 Peter was written on papyrus sometime between the years 200 and 300 AD.

Peter, James, and John witnessed the transfiguration of Jesus on a mountain, perhaps Mt. Hermon, in this region (Matt. 17:1–9).

In the region of Caesarea Philippi, Peter acknowledged Jesus as Lord (Matt. 16:13–16).

Born at Bethsaida, Peter was called from his fishing nets on the Sea of Galilee to become Jesus's disciple (John 1:44; Luke 5:1–11).

Beginning at Caesarea, Peter traveled through Judea and Samaria, proclaiming Christ and witnessing to the Gentiles (Acts 10:24—11:18).

A bold witness in the early church at Jerusalem (Acts 2:14–41), Peter broadened his witness to include the Gentiles following a vision on the rooftop of Simon the tanner in Joppa (Acts 10:9–23).

Peter denied Jesus three times on the night before his crucifixion (Matt. 26:69–75).

After his resurrection, Jesus appeared to Peter and the other disciples in the Upper Room in Jerusalem (Luke 24:33–43).

Tyre
Mt. Hermon
Caesarea Philippi
Mediterranean Sea
Ptolemais
Capernaum
Bethsaida (Galilee)
Magdala
Sea of Galilee
Cana of Galilee
Tiberias
Mt. Tabor
Yarmuk R.
Nazareth
Nain
Caesarea
Jordan R.
Mt. Gerizim
Sychar
Jabbok R.
Joppa
Emmaus
Jerusalem
Mt. of Olives
Jericho
Bethany
Bethlehem
Dead Sea

0    10 km.
0    10 miles

Public domain

**127**

# 1 John

John was close to Jesus. In the gospel of John, he called himself the disciple whom Jesus loved. This didn't mean Jesus loved John more than the other disciples—God loves everyone the same. But it does mean John felt a special closeness to Jesus. In this letter, John wants every believer to feel this same close relationship with Jesus.

## The Truth

John lived until the end of the first century AD. By that time, some people were spreading false teachings. One lie was that Jesus was a spiritual idea instead of a real person. Another lie was that Christians didn't have to obey the Ten Commandments or live a moral life. John wrote this letter to teach Christians the truth about Jesus and the importance of obeying the Bible.

## Who God Is

John wanted everyone in the church to know Jesus better. As you read through this book, look for these descriptions of who Jesus is. (Hint: Jesus is God!)

1. God is the word of life. Jesus loves us so much he wants to spend forever with us. That's why he came, died for our sins, and rose again—to offer us the gift of eternal life.

2. God is light. There is no darkness or evil in God.

3. God is just and is always fair. He punishes what is wrong or evil and rewards what is right or good.

4. God is righteous. Jesus is the final sacrifice for our sins. He died to pay the punishment for the wrong things we have done.

5. God is love. Everything God does is because of his perfect love for us, even if we don't understand it. God loves us and wants us to love each other.

6. God is truth. People might tell us confusing lies. But if we listen to God and read the Bible, we can know what the truth is.

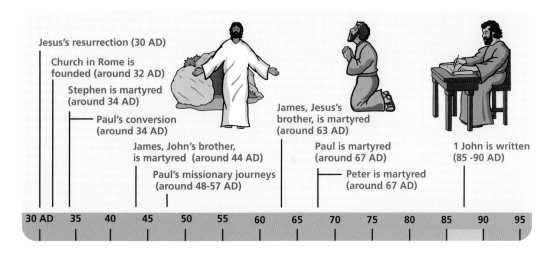

Jesus's resurrection (30 AD)

Church in Rome is
founded (around 32 AD)

Stephen is martyred
(around 34 AD)

Paul's conversion
(around 34 AD)

James, Jesus's
brother, is martyred
(around 63 AD)

James, John's brother,
is martyred (around 44 AD)

Paul is martyred
(around 67 AD)

1 John is written
(85 -90 AD)

Paul's missionary journeys
(around 48-57 AD)

Peter is martyred
(around 67 AD)

| 30 AD | 35 | 40 | 45 | 50 | 55 | 60 | 65 | 70 | 75 | 80 | 85 | 90 | 95 |

## Eyewitness Experience

John knew Jesus. They ate meals together. They walked together from town to town. John was with Jesus when Jesus healed the sick and fed the five thousand. He stood at the cross and saw Jesus crucified. Later, John looked inside the empty tomb. John talked with Jesus after Jesus came alive again! Just like the other disciples, John was an eyewitness to many of the things Jesus said and did. That's how he knew some people were spreading lies about Jesus. John had been with Jesus every step of his ministry and knew the truth about his teachings.

## The Apostle John

Jesus died and came to life again around 30–33 AD. His disciples carried on his ministry and the church grew. One by one, however, the disciples, Paul, and other leaders of the early church were martyred (killed) for their faith. Except for John. He outlived them all! John wrote this letter around 85–90 AD, just before he wrote the book of Revelation. The timeline at the top of the page shows some of the key events in the church that John lived through.

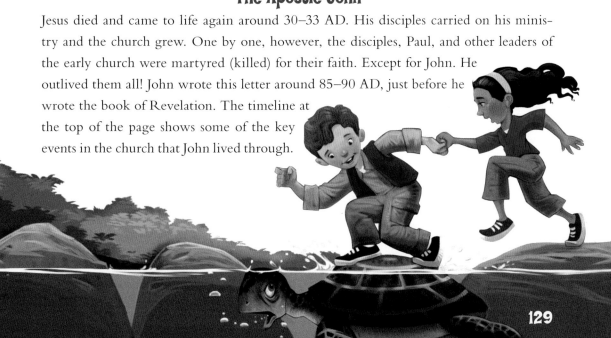

# 2 John

In his second letter, John warns Christians in the early church about the wrong ideas and false teachings that were being taught by people who did not accept the true teachings of Jesus. John's message to the church was written two thousand years ago. So what would John's message be to us today? Don't watch teachers on TV who say things that go against what the Bible says. Don't read their books. Don't follow them on social media. Instead, read the Bible to learn about what Jesus really taught. And be sure to go to a church that teaches the truth found in the Bible.

## Important Bible Words

In John's greeting, he sends "grace, mercy and peace from God the Father and from Jesus Christ." What do these words mean, especially when they come to us from God?

**Grace:** God's grace is kindness and love shown to someone who doesn't deserve it. God's ultimate grace came when Jesus offered the free gift of eternal life to anyone who follows him as Lord and Savior.

**Mercy:** God's mercy is the act of forgiving someone who is guilty. God showed us mercy when he offered his very own Son on the cross as a sacrifice for our sin.

**Peace:** God's peace is different than the world's peace. It can be confidence and trust in God and his promises, even when things don't look good or hopeful.

John may have walked down this street in Ephesus, which has been rebuilt from long ago.

According to some church traditions, John wrote 1, 2, and 3 John while living in the ancient city of Ephesus. He wrote the book of Revelation, which contains the visions he had on the nearby island of Patmos.

Nejdet Duzen/Shutterstock.com

This is the site of the church that is thought to have marked John's tomb in Ephesus.

## What Does Love Look Like?

As a disciple, John followed Jesus and listened to him teach. John heard Jesus say that the greatest commandment is to love God with all our heart, soul, and mind. Jesus also said that the second greatest commandment is to love our neighbor as ourselves. In this letter, John explained what love looks like. Real love means walking in obedience to God's commands. What is God's great command? For each of us to walk in love.

# 3 John

John felt toward Christians as a parent feels toward a child. He even called other believers his children. As a spiritual father, his greatest joy was to hear that people in the church were walking in the truth. Third John was originally written as a letter. In it, John told his friend Gaius it gave him joy to hear about Gaius's commitment to truth.

## Short but Powerful

This book is the shortest book in the entire Bible! And 2 John is only a little bit longer. Why are these books so short? Because they were both originally letters that were short enough to fit on one sheet of papyrus. Before he said good-bye in both letters, John explained that he kept his message short because he hoped to visit soon.

## Mail Delivery in Bible Times

How did mail get delivered in Bible times? Most likely, John would have asked someone who was already traveling that way to carry his letter along. This letter was probably hand-delivered by Demetrius, whom John praises near the end.

### Follow the Leader!

Truth was very important to John. As you read this book, look for ways John explains Christians can walk in truth.

1. Faithfully read the Bible and hold truth in our heart.

2. Do acts of kindness and love for other believers.

3. Welcome and support Christians and missionaries in their ministry.

4. Imitate what is good.

5. Share the truth about Jesus and the gospel with others.

6. Tell others about the good things Jesus has done for us.

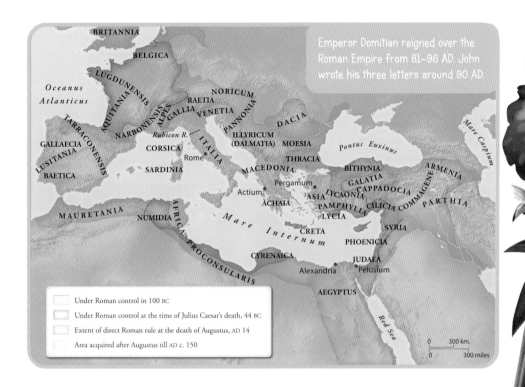

Emperor Domitian reigned over the Roman Empire from 81–96 AD. John wrote his three letters around 90 AD.

Under Roman control in 100 BC

Under Roman control at the time of Julius Caesar's death, 44 BC

Extent of direct Roman rule at the death of Augustus, AD 14

Area acquired after Augustus till AD c. 150

0    300 km.
0    300 miles

## Emperor Domitian

Tradition says John lived in the city of Ephesus in his later years. A temple was built there to honor Emperor Domitian. He was one of the emperors who demanded people worship him, persecuting Christians and others who refused. Domitian banished John to the island of Patmos because John taught about Jesus. Before John left for Patmos, however, he wrote this letter from Ephesus.

## Your Testimony

Each of us have a testimony—or story—to tell about how knowing Jesus makes a difference in our lives. Sometimes we share our testimony in words, other times we share it through the things we do. Can people tell you love Jesus by what you do and say? If someone you know were to visit John today, what would they tell him about your testimony?

John may have written with a pen similar to this ancient one used during the Roman Empire.

Metropolitan Museum of Art/Public Domain.

# Jude

Like many other books in the New Testament, the book of Jude was a letter. It was a warning against false teachings, because people were teaching that Jesus wasn't God. They also taught that God's grace gave them permission to sin and do wrong things. Jude reminded Christians everywhere to hold on to the truth of the gospel and reject every lie.

iStock.com/sedmak

Jude reminded the early believers to hold fast to the true gospel taught by the apostles of Jesus Christ.

## Meet Jude!

Who wrote this book? Jude identified himself as the brother of James, who was the leader of the early church in Jerusalem and wrote the book of James. He was also Jesus's half brother. This means Jude was Jesus's half brother too.

## Exercise

Push-ups. Sit ups. Jumping jacks. These are exercises people do to get in shape. In this book, Jude teaches us how to get our spiritual muscles in shape. Here is a list of exercises Jude recommends. Pray and ask God to show you how to practice each one.

- Build up your faith.
- Pray in the Holy Spirit.
- Keep yourself in God's love.
- Look to Jesus to save you.
- Look forward to spending eternity in heaven with God.
- Invite others to know Jesus too.

GERMANIA
Colonia
BELGICA INFERIOR
Augusta
Treverorum
GALLIA
RAETIA
NORICUM
Atlantic
Ocean
Lugdunum
Vienne
AQUITANIA
PANNONIA
DACIA
NARBONENSIS
Salona
MOESIA
ITALIA
Adriatic Sea
HISPANIA
Rome
THRACE Anchialus
Black Sea
MACEDONIA
Debeltum
Cumae
Thessalonica
Philippi
Amastris
Sinope
Puteoli Neapolis
Berea
Nicomedia
Tyrrhenian Sea
Larissa
Parium
Ancyra
Corduba
Nicopolis
Pergamum
Thyatira
Caesarea
Sardis
Philomelium
(Mazaca)
ACHAIA
Smyrna
Eumenia
Thuburba
Ephesus
Iconium
Cirta
Carthage
Lacedaemon
Magnesia
Apamea
Lystra
Derbe
NUMIDIA Uthina
Tralles
Perga
Alexandra
MAURETANIA
Madaurus
Laodicea Colossae
Attalia
Tarsus
Lambesis
Cnossus
Antioch
(Syrian)
Mediterranean Sea
Gortyna
Tripolis
SYRIA
Cyrene
Sidon
Damascus
Tyre
Bostra
Caesarea
Capernaum
CYRENAICA
Ptolemais
Joppa
Alexandria
Azotus
Jerusalem
LIBYA
Lydda
ARABIA
EGYPT
Red Sea

Extent of Christian Church, 1st century AD
• Significant Christian community, 1st century AD
Extent of Christian Church, 2nd century AD
◇ Significant Christian community, 2nd century AD
◆ Significant Christian community in both 1st and 2nd centuries

0   300 km.
0   300 miles

# Jesus's Family

You can read more about Jesus's family in other books in the New Testament. Mark 6:3 and Matthew 13:55–56 list the names of the brothers of Jesus and say Jesus had sisters too. John 7:5 tells us that his brothers did not believe Jesus was God. Yet Jude introduces himself as the servant of Jesus Christ. When did Jude change his mind about who Jesus really is? Most likely it happened when Jude saw Jesus after he died and came alive again. Acts 1:14 says that after Jesus's resurrection, his brothers and his mother were with the first Christians who met together in prayer. Jude and his family were eyewitnesses to the resurrected Jesus, the Savior. Only God could do the miraculous things Jesus did, so they knew that Jesus was God!

# Revelation

The apostle John wrote the book of Revelation after he was sent as a prisoner to the island of Patmos. Revelation is a book with three main parts. The first part explains who the message in this book is from . . . Jesus! The second part has seven messages for seven churches in New Testament times. The third part is a look ahead to the final phase of God's eternal plan. This part includes how God will conquer evil and live with his children forever in a new heaven and a new earth.

## The Sin Solution

Revelation tells us the end of God's big plan—which is really the beginning of a wonderful new life for his children. In Genesis, we see how sin first entered God's perfect world, and God's plan started. The Old Testament gives the Ten Commandments and explains the sin God does not want us to do. The New Testament tells how Jesus died and rose again to pay the penalty for our sin. Revelation shows how Jesus will conquer Satan and end the problem of sin forever. Hallelujah!

The Bible says Jesus will come back to Jerusalem through the Eastern Gate. Years ago, Arab leaders closed this gate with large stones in hope that this prophecy will not come true.

Revelation says Jesus will return to rule the earth as King of kings and Lord of lords.

## A Look at the Future

Revelation talks about things that will occur as part of the end times—the period between Jesus leaving earth and when he comes back. John wrote this book to let Christians know God had given him a vision of what was happening to the world then and what would happen to the world in the future, so we can be sure that everything is under God's control even when things look frightening or bad. But a lot of what John wrote down can also sound confusing, because God was showing him things using symbols and ideas that we won't totally understand until we see God in person. So don't worry if you don't grasp everything

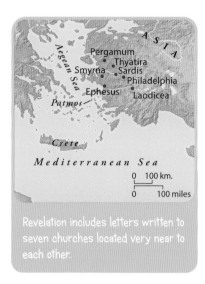

Revelation includes letters written to seven churches located very near to each other.

that happens in Revelation. Even Bible scholars have different thoughts about things God showed John. Just remember, God has it all planned out and will make everything perfect in the end!

### Seven Steps to Take

The letters to the churches in Bible times help our churches today. They remind us to:

1. Love Jesus with our whole heart.
2. Not be afraid of persecution.
3. Repent and stay true to the teachings of Jesus.
4. Do what is right and good.
5. Be strong in our faith.
6. Keep God's Word.
7. Treasure God's riches, not the world's.

## Prepare for His Coming

Revelation is the last book in the Bible. It tells what the end will be like when Jesus comes back to earth. We don't know when that will happen, but we can prepare our hearts for his return. We can choose to believe in Jesus. We can ask Jesus to be Lord of our lives. When he comes as King of kings, he will set up his kingdom and our new, forever life with him!

# References

## Numbers

1. https://www.rome2rio.com/map/Jericho/Mount-Sinai-Egypt#r/Bus-taxi.

   eNotes. "How many miles is it from Mt. Sinai (traditional site) to Jericho?" Accessed November 22, 2022. https://www.enotes.com/homework-help/1-how-many-miles-from-mt-sinai-traditional-site-303026. The approximate 345 miles assumes Mt. Sinai was what is now called Mt. Catherine in Egypt, a traditionally recognized location.

## Obadiah

1. All About Archaeology. "Herod the Great." Accessed October 8, 2022. https://www.allaboutarchaeology.org/herod-the-great.htm.

   Bible Ask. "Was King Herod From Esau's Lineage?" March 4, 2018. https://bibleask.org/king-herod-esaus-lineage/.

   Youngblood, Ronald F. *Nelson's Illustrated Bible Dictionary*. Nashville: Thomas Nelson, 2014, page 501.

   "Antiquities of the Jews, 1.1-2." The Works of Flavius Josephus. October 8, 2022. https://www.sacred-texts.com/jud/josephus/ant-2.htm.

2. UNESCO World Heritage Convention. "Petra." Accessed October 16, 2022. https://whc.unesco.org/en/list/326.

# Adventure BIBLE

**Take your young explorer on an adventure through God's Word with the #1 Bible for kids!**

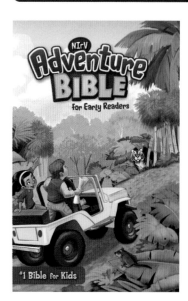

NIrV Adventure Bible
for Early Readers
9780310727422

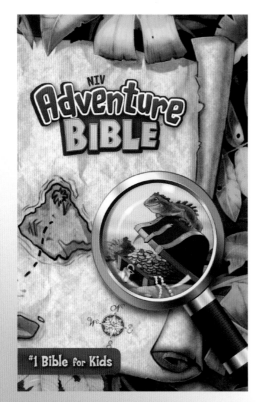

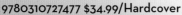

9780310727477 $34.99/Hardcover

The bestselling NIV Adventure Bible will get kids excited about reading the Scriptures! Your kids will be captivated with the full-color features that make it fun and engaging to read the Bible and memorize their favorite verses.